Perceptions of Libraries, 2010

Context and Community

A REPORT TO THE OCLC MEMBERSHIP

Perceptions of Libraries, 2010

Context and Community

A REPORT TO THE OCLC MEMBERSHIP

Principal contributors

Cathy De Rosa, MBA, Vice President for the Americas and Global Vice President of Marketing

Joanne Cantrell, Marketing Analyst

Matthew Carlson, Design Lead

Peggy Gallagher, MLS, MMC, Manager, Market Analysis

Janet Hawk, MBA, Director, Market Analysis & Sales Programs

Charlotte Sturtz, MBA, Campaign Analyst

Editing

Brad Gauder, Editor

Contributors

Diane Cellentani, MBA, Market Research Consultant to OCLC

Tam Dalrymple, MLS, Senior Information Specialist

Larry Olszewski, PhD, MLS, Director, OCLC Library

OCLC
Dublin, Ohio USA

Photography and art are copyright their respective sources:
iStockphoto.com: Cover, 3, 4, 11, 17, 18, 19, 21, 31, 32, 35, 39, 45, 54, 60, 63, 64, 65, 71, 73, 85, 92, 102
ThinkstockPhotos.com: 19, 24, 42, 47, 53, 58, 61, 67, 69, 75, 77, 79, 81, 83, 87, 89

Printed in the United States of America
Cataloged in WorldCat® on January 19, 2011

OCLC Control Number: 697520571
ISBN: 1-55653-395-0
        978-1-55653-395-2

15 14 13 12 11 10 | 1 2 3 4 5 6

TABLE OF CONTENTS

Much has changed in the environment since OCLC published *Perceptions of Libraries and Information Resources* in 2005. America has seen one of the worst recessions in its history, and there have been advances in technology. How these and other changes in the environment have affected the perceptions and use of information resources and the library is the focus of the first section of our report.

Perceptions and use of information resources and the library vary at different stages in life. What we have learned about libraries, communities and age is the focus of the second section of our report.

A Long View— In Internet Time

Eight years ago, my colleagues and I began work on our first OCLC membership report, *The 2003 OCLC Environmental Scan: Pattern Recognition*. Our aim was to learn about the attitudes and habits of the emerging "online information consumer." We explored three themes that described the information environment of the early Internet: self-service (moving to self-sufficiency), satisfaction and seamlessness. While that work barely scratched the surface of what we needed to explore, it set into motion community discussion and a series of OCLC studies aimed at learning more about the increasingly confident, empowered "information consumer."

Now we are releasing our fifth membership report, chronicling the online practices and perceptions of the 2010 information consumer. Previous OCLC membership reports include: *Perceptions of Libraries and Information Resources* in 2005; its companion report, *College Students' Perceptions of Libraries and Information Resources* in 2006; *Sharing, Privacy and Trust in Our Networked World* in 2007; *From Awareness to Funding: A study of library funding in America* in 2008; and today, *Perceptions of Libraries, 2010: Context and Community*.

While each study had a unique theme as we researched the hot topics of the time, the reports share a common goal—to provide a future frame for libraries by studying the perceptions, not just the practices, of the information consumer. Understanding beliefs over behaviors has been our primary research objective. If it is true that perception is reality or, maybe more accurately, perception predicts tomorrow's reality, then our goal has been to provide hard data about the current perceptions of the library, Internet and information, and the ties among the three. We have explored the physical library, the online library, search engines, searching,

> If perception is reality or, more accurately, perception predicts tomorrow's reality, then our goal has been to provide hard data about the current perceptions of the information consumer.

Internet privacy, trust, social networking, library funding and the concept of "library value." We have pushed hard to understand more about the information consumer's perception of the library brand.

We have assembled a rich set of information about the 21st century American information consumer. To our knowledge, it is the only data set collected about the Internet-era library user that documents his uses and perceptions of the library and online information. Some might argue that it is too early to have any sort of "long view" of the Internet information consumer. I would suggest that in Internet years, eight years is an information generation. But whether it is simply an eight-year view or indeed a preview to permanent change, important trends, shifting perceptions and new hot spots have emerged that we believe will shape the future landscape for libraries.

For libraries, this long view presents challenges—and opportunities.

Cathy De Rosa
Vice President for the Americas and
Global Vice President of Marketing
OCLC

Information Consumers: 2003–2010

Before we move into what surfaced in our 2010 work, a brief summary of our earlier studies and a few thoughts about economic context are useful.

2003

We met the information consumer as he was beginning to experience the power of the Internet. He may have been buying a book on Amazon, Web "surfing" or e-mailing on Yahoo! Most information consumers had been online only for a few years, except for those under age 25 and librarians who had more experience.

The credibility of information resulting from search engines was a hot debate in the library community. The information consumer was not at all concerned. Fourteen million U.S. consumers made an online purchase in 2002, totaling $1.3 billion. Sixty-five percent (65%) of college students reported that they played video, computer or online games.

In September 2003, Google turned five years old. Google Answers was launched. Blogs and wikis were the newest collaboration technologies. Gartner Group predicted that corporate blogs were five to ten years into the future.

2005

The majority of online information consumers (82%) began their searches for information on a search engine, a source they found roughly as trustworthy as a library. One percent (1%) began their searches on a library Web site.

The information consumer loved search engines, with a favorability rating over 85%. They also loved librarians, with 76% of those assisted by a librarian indicating the librarian adds value to the search process. The information consumer was very confident of his information searching skills. If in doubt of the results, he just checked another Web site.

2003 Hot Spots

 34% of Internet users were seniors, age 65+.

 Library e-content purchases were just taking off. 2% of U.S. library funding was spent on e-content and electronic subscriptions.

 Search engine results were being debated. 78% of Outsell survey respondents said the Web was providing "most of what they needed."

2005 Hot Spots

 Libraries played many community roles. Americans felt libraries were a place to learn (83%) and offered free computer and Internet access (75%).

 Information searches began on search engines. The majority of Americans were satisfied with their most recent search experience on a search engine (91%).

 Search engines were a favorite. More than half of Americans (54%) felt search engines were a perfect fit for their lifestyles. 18% felt the same about libraries.

The top method for learning about a new electronic information resource was from a friend (58%), with links from another Web resource (55%) second. The information consumer was not willing to pay for information, but he was getting very comfortable with making online purchases.

Ninety-six percent (96%) of online information consumers had visited a library at sometime in the past, with 1% visiting the day before they took the survey. Seventy-five percent (75%) of American information consumers had a library card. They predicted that their use of the library would remain steady over the next three to five years—and our 2010 results indicate that their predictions were correct.

Each year from 2003 to 2007, the U.S. economy grew. The positive effects of economic growth were everywhere, it seemed, except at the public library.

In 2005, over a third of U.S. public libraries reported declining budgets. Library levies were struggling. Seventy-five percent (75%) of library operating levies passed in the mid-1990s; by 2005, the pass rate for operating levies had slipped to under 60%. It seemed the library "value" was less clear to voters in the strong economic Internet world. The library was certainly a nice institution to have, but library directors frequently fielded questions from community leaders and elected officials about the future role of the library "when we have Google." U.S. university library budgets remained stable.

2007

The term social networking had been coined. Thirty-seven percent (37%) of online information consumers were using social networks. MySpace led the social networking sites with 75% market share; next were Classmates.com and Facebook at 31% each. College students were connecting on their own social site, Facebook, which had just opened beyond the college student audience. Less than 10% of information consumers thought it was the library's role to build a social site, and librarians agreed.

While futurists were predicting security breaches and privacy erosion, the information consumer was not worried. He was not afraid to share information—with friends, new online friends, libraries or commercial organizations. The information consumer, not commercial organizations or libraries, was defining what should be private.

Search engine penetration among information consumers approached saturation, with 86% using search engines, up from 71% in 2005. Yahoo! was the top global Web site. Amazon was the top commercial Web site in the U.S. Ninety-two percent (92%) of librarians used Amazon; 21% used it daily. Google was the most-used search engine. YouTube was the fastest growing Web site, followed by Facebook.

About sixty percent (59%) of information consumers had used instant messaging, and 20% of information consumers had created a Web page. The number-one reason for creating a Web page was to communicate with family and friends. Cell phone ringtones were hot, a $550 million dollar business (BMI, March 2008).

Sixty-three percent (63%) of information consumers had a library card.

2010

The U.S. economic boom was replaced by what has been called "The Great Recession" (*New York Times*, March 2009). In January 2010 when we conducted the most recent study, the U.S. unemployment rate topped 9.8% (U.S. Bureau of Labor Statistics, February 2010). It remains at over 9% in January 2011. The number of Americans who had experienced a negative job impact (lost a job, had to take a job at a lower salary, worked a second job, etc.) during the recession was even larger. Our research shows that the number is double the unemployment rate, at 20%. A third of American families had at least one family member who experienced a negative job impact during the recession.

2007 Hot Spots

Social networking was growing. 41% of Americans were extremely or very familiar with social networking sites.

Online privacy was debated, although more than half of social media users (55%) had shared photos on a social media site.

Most online Americans (91%) had used the Internet for over four years.

Cell phone use was up. 41% of American cell phone users were texting and 20% had downloaded ringtones.

2010 Hot Spots

The Great Recession impacted the U.S. The unemployment rate topped 9.8%. Even more Americans—20%—had experienced a negative job impact.

Mobile phones increase in popularity. 23% of U.S. mobile phones are smartphones providing Internet access.

All ages are connected. Over 90% of Boomers use e-mail and search engines. Over 50% use a social networking site.

While the economy was declining, the online activities of the information consumer were increasing. Seventy-seven percent (77%) of Americans were online, up 12% from 2005 (Internet World Stats, September 2010). comScore reported that a quarter of U.S. mobile phones are now smartphones that provide Internet access, a growth of 1,050% from 2005. Many of the online practices of young information consumers in 2005 were across all ages in 2010. Over 90% of Boomers used e-mail and search engines, and over 50% used a social networking site.

In 2010, 68% of information consumers had a library card. For those Americans economically impacted, that rate was even higher—81%. Information consumers who have experienced a job impact were not just getting library cards at greater rates; they were using the library for more services and more often in 2010. And their perception of library value was significantly different from those not impacted—their perceived value was higher.

Today and beyond

Perceptions of Libraries, 2010: Context and Community reports the changes and evolutions in the information consumer's life in the last five years, with particular attention given to the actions, attitudes and perceptions observed in 2005. We know from other research that The Great Recession has reshaped attitudes and practices in many lifestyle areas, and we wanted to better understand the impact on the information consumer's use of online information and the library. We studied the differences and similarities between information consumers who had experienced a negative job impact in the recession and those who did not. And as the "digital age divide" becomes less distinct, we turned our attention to better understanding if the attitudes of the 2010 information consumer were now ageless or if age differences still played a distinct role in how we perceive and use information— and libraries.

In Context

Much has changed in the environment since OCLC published *Perceptions of Libraries and Information Resources* in 2005. There have been leaps in consumer technology and services, and America has seen one of the worst recessions in its history.

Some of today's most popular social Internet sites were either just starting up (Facebook) or did not even exist (Twitter) in 2005. Smartphones had just barely broken into the marketplace, and the popular Kindle e-book reader was still two years away. Technology advances touched libraries as well with more than 80% of U.S. public libraries now offering wireless access to the Internet.

As Americans have embraced advancements in technology over the past five years, they have also been hit by The Great Recession, a U.S. economy plagued by the highest unemployment rates in decades and significant losses in wealth, real estate and retirement savings. Americans even beyond the almost 10% who are unemployed have been negatively impacted by the poor economy. They are making lifestyle adjustments such as reduced spending and saving, and they are using libraries more—a lot more!

Not only are Americans using the library and its many services more, they also see increased value of the library for themselves and for their communities. They agree—overwhelmingly—that librarians are valuable. And they believe—overwhelmingly—that libraries equal books.

We put what we learned into context.

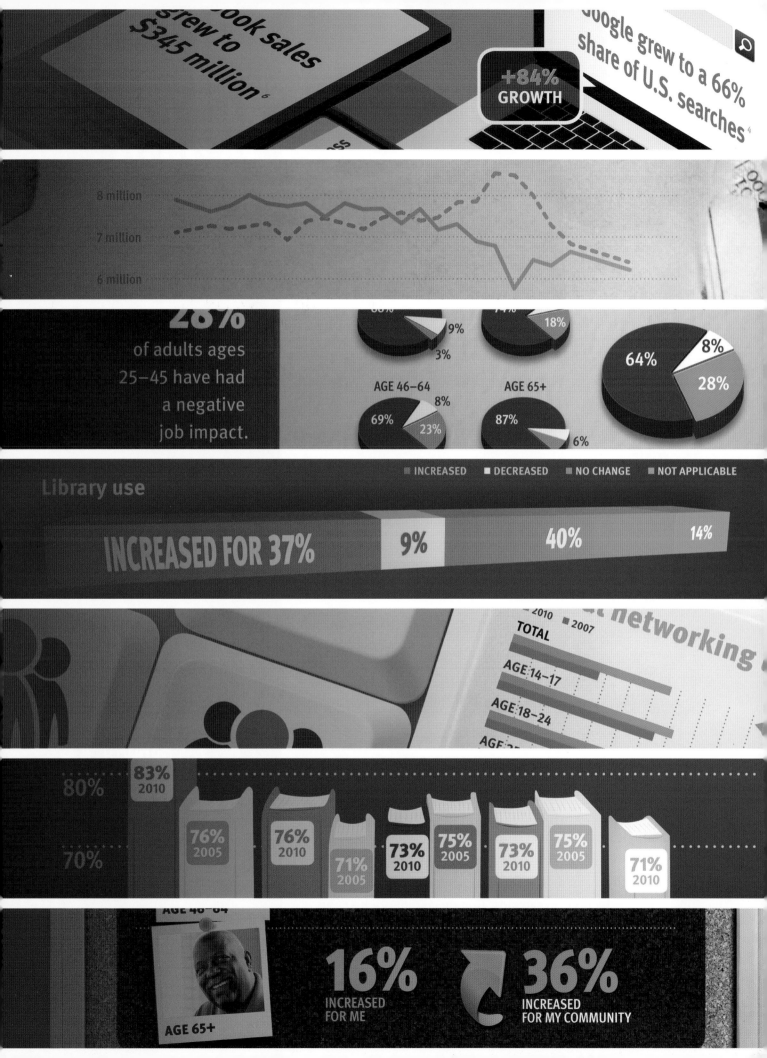

ook sales grew to $345 million [6]

+84% GROWTH

Google grew to a 66% share of U.S. searches [4]

8 million
7 million
6 million

28% of adults ages 25–45 have had a negative job impact.

9%
3%
18%
8%
64%
28%

AGE 46–64
69%
8%
23%

AGE 65+
87%
6%

Library use

■ INCREASED ■ DECREASED ■ NO CHANGE ■ NOT APPLICABLE

INCREASED FOR 37%   9%   40%   14%

networking

■ 2010 ■ 2007

TOTAL
AGE 14–17
AGE 18–24
AGE

80%
83% 2010
76% 2005
76% 2010
73% 2010
75% 2005
73% 2010
75% 2005

70%
71% 2005
71% 2010

AGE 46–64

AGE 65+

16% INCREASED FOR ME

36% INCREASED FOR MY COMMUNITY

From 2005 to 2010...

...technology growth in the U.S.

What a difference five years make. In 2005 when OCLC published *Perceptions of Libraries and Information Resources*, information consumers had one primary means to access the Internet—the PC—and "social networking" was not yet an acknowledged term. Facebook was limited to college and high school students; YouTube had just been launched; no one was tweeting; the Kindle was not available; and there were no iPhones nor iPhone applications. Today's technology landscape is a much more social and crowded consumer space. The information consumer has multiple devices, new platforms and a seemingly infinite number of ways to interact with other information consumers.

Searching

According to Internet World Stats, more than two-thirds of Americans were online in 2005—69% had Internet access. Today, more than three-fourths (77%), or 239 million Americans, are online, a 12% growth in five years.

While hardware and services have seen many new entrants since 2005, information consumers' top choice in search engines remains Google. In 2005, more than a third of U.S. searches were conducted using Google, followed closely by the use of Yahoo! sites (comScore, August 2006). Now, two-thirds of searches are conducted through Google, according to comScore (December 2010), an 84% growth. Sixteen percent (16%) are conducted through Yahoo! sites. To remain on top, Google has released many new services in the past five years including Gmail, Google Docs, Google Books, Google News and Google Apps. *The Wall Street Journal* (September 2010) reports that with Google's search engine upgrade, Google Instant, time spent searching could be reduced by as much as five seconds (or 20%) from the average 25 seconds. Google Instant predicts the searcher's term as he types, designed to provide "search at the speed of thought."

+1,544% GROWTH

Sources
1. comScore, December 21, 2010
2. ALA, June 2010
3. Internet World Stats, September 2010
4. comScore, December 15, 2010
5. OCLC, 2011
6. Association of American Publishers, December 2010

+1,300% GROWTH

Facebook grew to 152 million U.S. unique monthly visitors[1]

Wireless Internet at public libraries grew to 82%[2]

+12% GROWTH

+116% GROWTH

239 million Americans are online[3]

E-book sales grew to $345 million[6]

Search

🔍

Google grew to a 66% share of U.S. searches[4]

+84% GROWTH

Mobile access to the Internet doubled to 11% of Americans[5]

+100% GROWTH

Socializing

Social networking was just emerging in 2005. Social media sites such as Flickr and YouTube were gaining traction, and the potential to share more than photos and videos was only beginning to unfold. Few usage statistics were available. By 2007, social networking was being discussed by the press as the next "new space" in online communities. The 2007 OCLC report, *Sharing, Privacy and Trust in Our Networked World,* identified that a third of Americans were exploring social networking (37%) and media sites (32%). These sites were primarily seen as sources for teens and young adults. Today, two-thirds of Americans, of all ages, are now using social sites. MySpace, YouTube and Facebook dominated in popularity among American survey respondents in 2007. Facebook, YouTube, MySpace, LinkedIn and Twitter (launched in July 2006) now lead the pack (*Wireless and Mobile News*, October 2010). Twitter, with 24 million U.S. unique monthly visitors in late 2010, has seen 1,100% growth since 2007, according to comScore data.

One of the most empowering services for the information consumer in the past five years has been Facebook. Launched in 2004, early users were required to be college students with a college/university (.edu) e-mail address. The service was expanded to high school students in 2005 and the door was opened to any participant age 13 and older in 2006. According to comScore data, Facebook has seen a growth of 1,300% from 2005 to 2010. Facebook surpassed Google

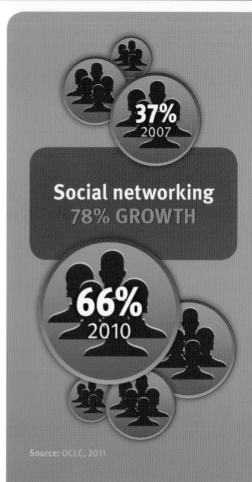

Social networking
78% GROWTH

37%
2007

66%
2010

Source: OCLC, 2011

Facebook surpassed Google as the most-visited site in March 2010 in the U.S.

Source: Hitwise, March 2010

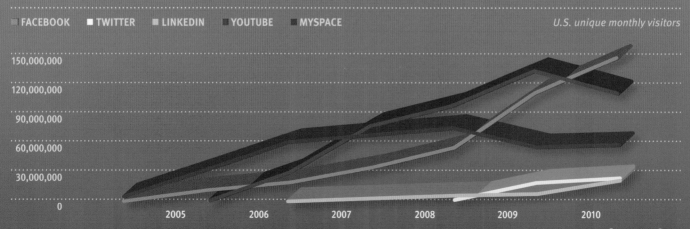

Social networking sites see exponential growth

■ FACEBOOK ■ TWITTER ■ LINKEDIN ■ YOUTUBE ■ MYSPACE

U.S. unique monthly visitors

150,000,000						
120,000,000						
90,000,000						
60,000,000						
30,000,000						
0						
	2005	2006	2007	2008	2009	2010

Source: comScore

1,050%
FIVE-YEAR GROWTH

**Smartphone
ownership**

2% in 2005
23% in 2010

Source: comScore,
September 2010

Smartphone shipments expected to exceed PCs in 2012.
Source: Morgan Stanley Research, June 2010

as the most-visited Web site in the U.S. in March 2010 (Hitwise, March 2010).

Mobile migration

Social networking is not unique in its exponential growth over the past half-decade. Cell phone penetration also surged. Two-thirds of Americans owned a cell phone in 2005. Today that number stands at 93% (CTIA, June 2010). The percentage of teens ages 12 to 17 who own a cell phone exploded from 45% in 2005 to 75% in 2010 (Pew, April 2010).

The big story in cell phone advancement may well be the growth in smartphone use—mobile phones that have functionality beyond contemporary cell phones and similar to that of personal computers, such as e-mail and Internet access. Just 2% of American cell phone subscribers owned a smartphone in 2005 (comScore, March 2005). comScore reports that 23%, or nearly 59 million Americans, now own a smartphone (September 2010). The rapid growth is projected to continue; so by 2012, shipments of smartphones are expected to exceed shipments of PCs (Morgan Stanley Research, June 2010).

How people are using cell phones also has evolved significantly. Texting is now a primary mode of communication among teens. In 2005, 74% of online teens preferred instant messaging (IM) as their primary means of connecting with friends; texting was second. These usage preferences have reversed. Texting is now favored by nearly 90% of teen cell phone owners (Pew, April 2010).

Beyond cell phones, mobility and wireless access also are changing the way the information consumer accesses the Internet. The rate of mobile adoption is outpacing prior Internet-based technologies.

80% of smartphone owners use apps
18 and older in the U.S.

Top apps: **Google Maps, Facebook**

Source: *Business Wire*, December 2010

According to the Burson-Marsteller blog (September 2010), the initial three-year growth rate of Apple's iPhone/iPod Touch, launched in June 2007, is ten times faster than the initial three-year growth rate of the online service AOL. Today, 40% of iPhone/iPod Touch users access the Internet with these devices more often than they do with their desktops or laptops.

Any discussion of the technology landscape in 2010 must include the rise of apps, downloadable software applications or programs used for specific tasks. According to a recent study conducted by Moosylvania, 80% of smartphone users age 18 and older use apps (*Business Wire*, December 2010).

According to CNET, the Apple Apps store has 300,000 apps, and the number of apps available for downloading increases daily. From just April–October 2010, the number of apps available in the Android market, owned by Google, doubled from 50,000 apps to 100,000 (*CNET News*, October 2010).

E-readers—redefining reading

Available since the early 1970s with the launch of Project Gutenberg, e-books and e-book readers (first introduced in the late 1990s with the Rocket eBook reader) are just now achieving consumer adoption. While hundreds of thousands of titles were available in 2005, adoption was low. The consumer appetite increased when Amazon released its now market-leading Kindle e-book reader in 2007. The first shipment of the Kindle sold out within hours. Just three years after the Kindle's debut, Amazon reported that customers purchased more Kindle e-books than hardcover print books during the three-month period of May–July 2010 (Amazon, July 2010).

Amazon may be leading the e-reader market with its Kindle, but other players in the e-book and e-book reader field have led to an e-book adoption tipping point. E-readers, including Barnes & Noble's Nook, Kobo, Sony Readers and Apple's iPad, have fueled the market for digital books. E-reader features include highlighting and note-taking, expanding the interactions between the reader and his book. Integrated links and embedded

44% of academic libraries and **34% of public libraries** offer mobile services...such as mobile connections to their Web sites and catalogs.
Source: *Library Journal*, October 2010

At current rate, the iPad will exceed **$9B** in U.S. sales [in 2011] and become the 4th biggest consumer electronics category.
Source: Bernstein Research, October 2010

In October 2010, Amazon.com's **Kindle e-books outsold best-selling print books** 2 to 1—for the first time.
Source: Amazon, October 25, 2010

More than 11% of all published books—two trillion words—have been scanned by Google.
Source: *The New York Times*, December 16, 2010

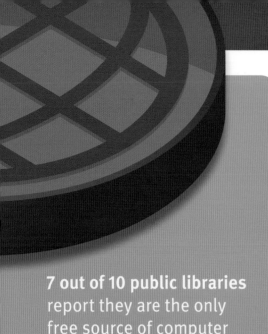

7 out of 10 public libraries report they are the only free source of computer and Internet access for their communities.

Source: ALA, June 2010

Most libraries now offer wireless Internet access

2005
37%
Source: ALA, 2006

2009
82%
Source: ALA, June 2010

1,010,000 videos on YouTube include "library," "libraries" or "librarians" in the title description.

Source: Search conducted on YouTube, January 2011

video are just the beginning of the social tools that will unlock the boundaries of the traditional book and redefine the act of reading. Today, 55% of public libraries offer e-books (ALA, April 2010).

Libraries in the technology landscape

The technology landscape that continues to empower information consumers has set new expectations for library users. Libraries are responding by offering new services and by joining the online social networks used by their information consumers. Eleven percent (11%) of larger U.S. public libraries have a Facebook site (ALA, April 2010). A search conducted in January 2011 identified more than 15,700 Facebook URLs that include the word "library." Libraries also have a growing presence on social media sites. In 2007, a YouTube search found 25,700 videos that included "library," "libraries" or "librarians." In January 2011, that number has rocketed to 1,010,000 videos, a 3,830% increase.

Libraries provide vital technology services to their users both outside and inside the library. Libraries are delivering services to their increasingly mobile communities by offering mobile connections to their Web sites and catalogs. Some are offering mobile ask-a-question services via text messaging. According to an October 2010 survey conducted by *Library Journal*, 44% of academic libraries and 34% of public libraries offer some type of mobile services.

According to the American Library Association's (ALA's) *Public Library Funding & Technology Access Study*, the number of public access computer stations in public libraries totaled over 230,000 or an average of 14 stations per library in 2009, up from 11 stations in 2005. The growth in the percentage of public libraries offering wireless Internet access has more than doubled from 38% in 2005 to 82% in 2009. A majority of public libraries, 67%, report that they are the only free source of computer and Internet access for the communities they serve.

Libraries are playing a central and increasingly critical role as technology providers for American information consumers.

THE GREAT RECESSION

Rising unemployment, declining consumer wealth, lower expectations

The U.S. economy has undergone tumultuous changes in the five years since the publication of OCLC's *Perceptions of Libraries and Information Resources* in 2005. The Great Recession began in December 2007 and officially ended in June 2009, according to the National Bureau of Economic Research. America experienced job losses, lingering high unemployment, reduced consumer confidence and significant losses in real estate, stock and retirement savings.

Unemployment defined the economy. Job losses exceeded job gains beginning in second quarter 2007 and peaking in first quarter 2009 with over 2.7 million lost jobs in that quarter. The U.S. unemployment rate peaked at 10.1% in October 2009—the first time it had been in double digits since 1983 (U.S. Bureau of Labor Statistics, January 2011).

Other employment factors were also negatively impacted. The average hours employed per work week dropped to 33, the lowest level since 1964 when the government first began collecting this data. Weekly wage increases declined sharply from an annual 3.4% increase in 2007 down to an annual 1.0% increase in 2009. The number of Americans employed only part-time grew 103% from 2007 to 2009 (U.S. Bureau of Labor Statistics, January 2011).

Americans sought relief in education. Americans went back to school and stayed in school. Seventy percent (70%) of the high school graduating class of 2009 were enrolled in college in October 2009, the highest percentage on record (back to 1959) according to the U.S. Bureau of Labor Statistics (April 2010).

Community colleges in particular played a critical role in helping Americans meet their educational goals. According to the Pew

> " I now live in a rural area without high speed internet. Using the library for things I used to be able to afford saves me so much and allows me to continue to read study and research without difficulty."
>
> **61-YEAR-OLD**

During The Great Recession...

...more jobs were lost than gained.

■ GROSS JOB GAINS ■ GROSS JOB LOSSES

9 million
8 million
7 million
6 million
5 million

2004   2005   2006   2007   2008   2009   2010

The Great Recession

...the annual unemployment rate more than doubled.

Year	Rate
2004	5.5%
2005	5.1%
2006	4.6%
2007	4.6%
2008	5.8%
2009	9.3%
2010	9.7%

10%
8%
6%
4%
2%

Source: U.S. Bureau of Labor Statistics

Research Center (October 2009), enrollments at community colleges grew by nearly 10% during the height of the recession while enrollments at four-year colleges remained stable. Community colleges offered students a less-expensive, more attainable alternative method of improving their skills in the tightest job market in a generation.

The Great Recession shifted Americans' work lives, home ownership, consumption and savings habits. The average annual expenditures per consumer fell 2.8% in 2009. This was the first time there had been a year-over-year drop in spending since the Consumer Expenditure Survey began publishing this data in 1984. Purchases for transportation, entertainment and apparel were among the major declines in consumer spending (U.S. Bureau of Labor Statistics, October 2010).

Bankruptcy filings rose 74% over the 24-month period ending June 30, 2009. A total of 1,306,315 bankruptcy cases were filed in federal courts in 2009 compared to 751,056 filed in 2007 (United States Courts, August 2010). Homes in foreclosure increased from a low of 1% in 2005 to a high of 4.58% in 2009 (Mortgage Bankers Association, 2009). Single-family housing completions have steadily declined since 2004. From 2005 to 2009, single-family housing completions dropped 215 percent (U.S. Census Bureau, June 2010). Housing prices dropped across the country. For many Americans, their homes were no longer assets or sources of financial security.

Small businesses struggled. U.S early-stage entrepreneurship declined 35% from 2005 to 2009, according to the Global Entrepreneurship Monitor. There were fewer business start-ups. Small business owners were less optimistic. Measures of their perceptions decreased 142% from 2007 to 2010 concerning their financial situation, revenue, cash flow, capital spending, number of jobs and ease of obtaining credit. (Wells Fargo/Gallup Small Business Index, August 2010).

Libraries play a critical role in the lives of Americans, even more so during down economic times.

Home foreclosures

358% INCREASE

(2005–2009) [1]

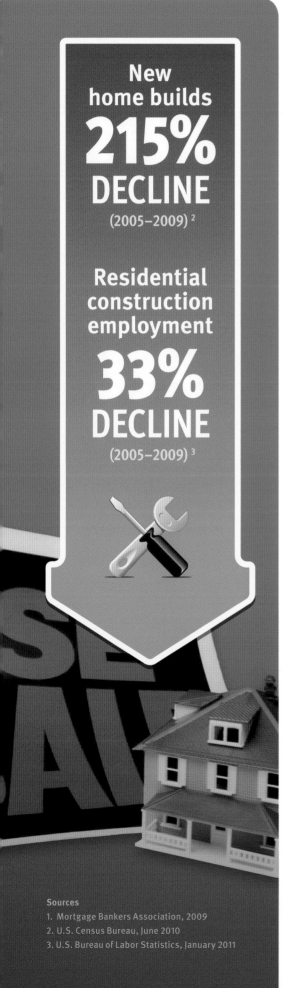

Sources
1. Mortgage Bankers Association, 2009
2. U.S. Census Bureau, June 2010
3. U.S. Bureau of Labor Statistics, January 2011

The American Library Association (ALA) reports increases in the number of people visiting libraries, checking out library materials and using library Internet terminals during the recession.

Public libraries provide critical assistance to job-seekers and small business owners and to those needing technology. OCLC's research reported in *How Libraries Stack Up, 2010* indicated that 300,000 Americans receive job-seeking help at public libraries every day—and 2.8 million times each month public libraries are used to support small businesses. Many libraries—5,400 public libraries, according to ALA—offer technology training classes.

At the same time that libraries often are seeing double-digit increases in the use of their services, many are experiencing budget cuts. In 2009–2010, the majority of public libraries (56%) had flat or decreased funding and 24 states reported cuts to their public library budgets (ALA, June 2010). In response to these funding cuts, some libraries have had to reduce their hours and close branches—making them less accessible at a time when they are even more needed. ALA reports that 15% of public libraries decreased their operating hours.

Lasting effects of the recession are yet to be seen

Americans' beliefs, values and consumer habits have seen dramatic shifts. As Gerzema and D'Antonio, authors of *Spend Shift: How the Post-Crisis Values Revolution is Changing the Way We Buy, Sell, and Live*, optimistically conclude, "In sacrificing, reimagining ourselves, and working harder, we have discovered we are stronger and more capable than we thought... The Great Recession has given us an unexpected gift, a renewed source of energy and determination to move forward." Americans are moving forward by making changes in their spending habits and lifestyle choices. They need access to resources to help learn new trades and find new jobs. And they need alternatives to entertainment they can no longer afford. They are turning to their library.

We'll explore the library's role during a down economy further in upcoming chapters.

ECONOMICALLY IMPACTED AMERICANS

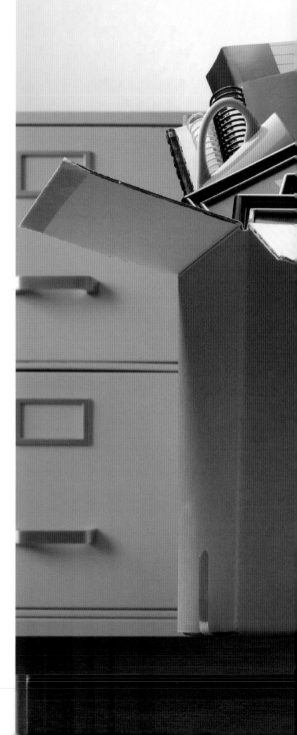

Americans are hit hard by the recession

The rise in unemployment is just one of the employment fallouts of the economic downturn. The U.S. Bureau of Labor Statistics reports that the current unemployment rate stands at 9.4% (December 2010), but our survey found that the negative employment impacts of the recent recession extended beyond unemployment for Americans. Twenty percent (20%) of those surveyed indicated that they had experienced a negative change to their employment status.

Given the extent of the employment impact on the American information consumer, we wanted to better understand the differences in attitudes, behaviors and perceptions, if any, that may exist between Americans whose employment was negatively impacted by the recent recession and those who had not experienced a job impact. We explored how a change in employment influences or impacts information use. We also studied how economically impacted Americans have changed their use, perceptions and attitudes about the library.

The economically impacted American

Survey data find 20% of Americans have had a negative employment impact—more than double the current unemployment rate. In this report, we define "economically impacted" as those Americans whose personal employment status has been adversely affected by the current economic environment, either from a job loss, a reduction in the hours employed, employment or reemployment at a lower wage, or taking on more than one job or additional hours to make ends meet. (The graphic on page 21 details the changes in job status that define "economically impacted.")

20% of Americans—twice the unemployment rate—have been economically impacted

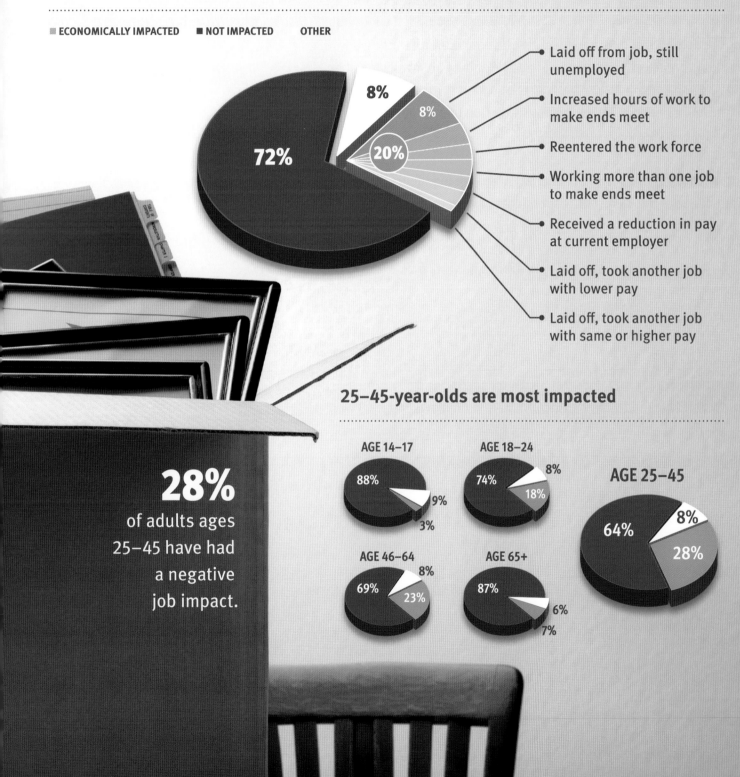

■ ECONOMICALLY IMPACTED   ■ NOT IMPACTED   OTHER

72%

8%

20%

8%

- Laid off from job, still unemployed
- Increased hours of work to make ends meet
- Reentered the work force
- Working more than one job to make ends meet
- Received a reduction in pay at current employer
- Laid off, took another job with lower pay
- Laid off, took another job with same or higher pay

25–45-year-olds are most impacted

28% of adults ages 25–45 have had a negative job impact.

AGE 14–17
88%
9%
3%

AGE 18–24
74%
8%
18%

AGE 25–45
64%
8%
28%

AGE 46–64
69%
8%
23%

AGE 65+
87%
6%
7%

A third of American families are impacted

Our survey also found that a significant number of the respondents, while not personally experiencing a change in job status, had immediate family members who had been impacted. If we combine the numbers of directly impacted respondents with those who were not economically impacted but had an immediate family member who was impacted, we find that over a third of all American families have likely experienced some negative job impact during the recent recession.

While we define "economically impacted" respondents in the balance of this report as respondents who were personally impacted, it is worth noting that the outcomes and attitudes that we report for the economically impacted segment of Americans may logically apply to an even broader household view.

Americans are concerned

Respondents, both directly impacted and those who have not experienced a job impact, shared similar concerns about their current livelihoods and future prosperity. Adults over age 18 were asked about their current attitudes toward finances, healthcare,

Over a third
of American families have experienced negative employment effects.

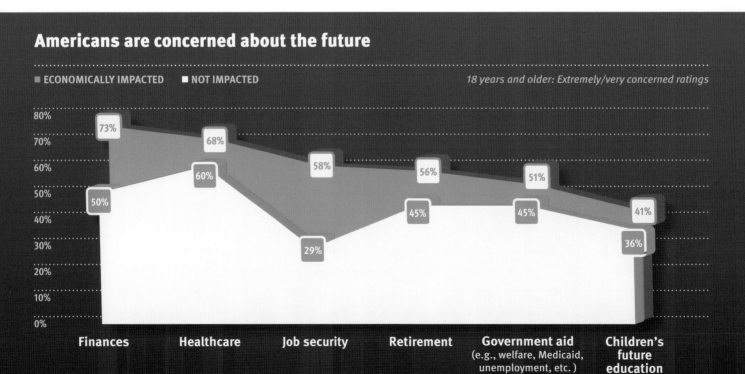

Americans are concerned about the future

■ ECONOMICALLY IMPACTED   ■ NOT IMPACTED   *18 years and older: Extremely/very concerned ratings*

	Finances	Healthcare	Job security	Retirement	Government aid (e.g., welfare, Medicaid, unemployment, etc.)	Children's future education
Economically impacted	73%	68%	58%	56%	51%	41%
Not impacted	50%	60%	29%	45%	45%	36%

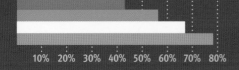

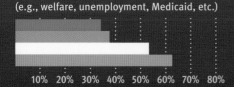
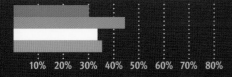
jobs, retirement, government aid and their children's education. Those impacted and those with no job impact are almost equally concerned about healthcare, the state of government aid (e.g., welfare, unemployment, Medicaid, etc.), and about funding their children's education. Healthcare is the highest concern (60%) for Americans not economically impacted. As expected, the largest differences are in the areas of job security and finances. While more than half (58%) of economically impacted Americans are concerned about job security, just 29% of those who had not experienced a change in job status are extremely or very concerned about job security. Seventy-three percent (73%) of the economically impacted are concerned about finances compared to 50% of those not impacted by the economy. This was the highest concern for the economically impacted.

Differences by age groups were also identified. Young adults, under age 25, are less concerned about finances than older Americans, but showed greater concern over job security, with more than 40% of younger Americans extremely or very concerned about jobs. Healthcare concerns increased with age as expected, but younger Americans are also concerned. Forty-two percent (42%) of younger adults have concerns about healthcare.

Concern about finances is more strongly expressed by Americans age 25 and older. Overall, 50 to 60% of Americans over age 24 are concerned about their finances. Similar patterns hold for this age group related to retirement concerns. About half of adults age 25 or older are concerned about retirement, with the 46–64-year-olds most concerned. Government aid concerns are expressed by all age groups, but concerns grow significantly for Americans over age 45.

More economically impacted Americans are online

Our survey data show that compared to those not impacted by the economy, impacted Americans are more likely to use a broader set of online resources. Social networking, online research, banking and bill paying are online activities the economically impacted are engaging in more extensively. Eighty percent (80%) of respondents who have had a job impact are engaged in social networking, compared to 64% of those not impacted. Seventy percent (70%)

Economically impacted Americans use library services more frequently

Monthly activities among library users

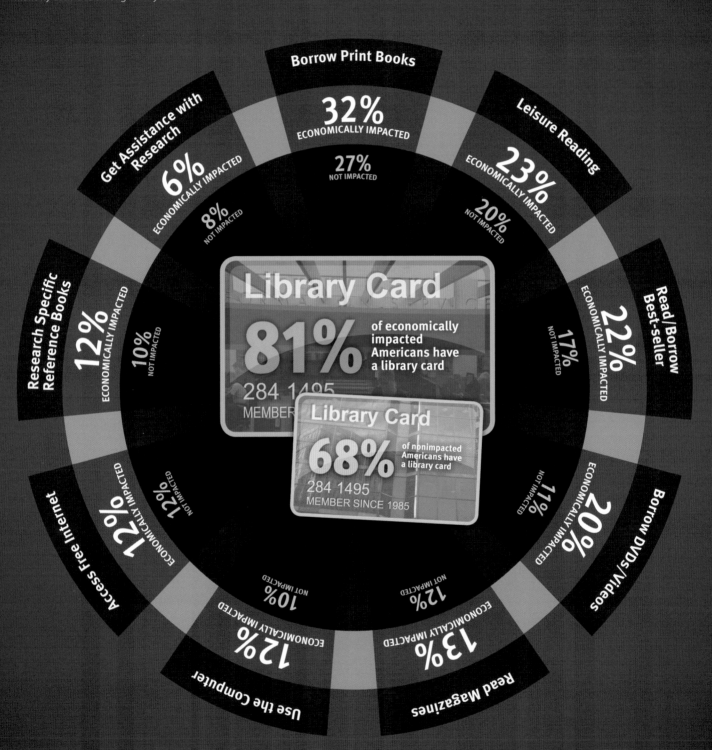

Borrow Print Books
32% ECONOMICALLY IMPACTED
27% NOT IMPACTED

Get Assistance with Research
6% ECONOMICALLY IMPACTED
8% NOT IMPACTED

Leisure Reading
23% ECONOMICALLY IMPACTED
20% NOT IMPACTED

Research Specific Reference Books
12% ECONOMICALLY IMPACTED
10% NOT IMPACTED

Read/Borrow Best-seller
22% ECONOMICALLY IMPACTED
17% NOT IMPACTED

Access Free Internet
12% ECONOMICALLY IMPACTED
12% NOT IMPACTED

Borrow DVDs/Videos
20% ECONOMICALLY IMPACTED
11% NOT IMPACTED

Use the Computer
12% ECONOMICALLY IMPACTED
10% NOT IMPACTED

Read Magazines
13% ECONOMICALLY IMPACTED
12% NOT IMPACTED

Library Card
81% of economically impacted Americans have a library card
284 1495 MEMBER

Library Card
68% of nonimpacted Americans have a library card
284 1495 MEMBER SINCE 1985

What are economically impacted Americans doing online?

They are more likely to engage in...

✓ Social networking	80%
✓ Research	74%
✓ Banking	73%
✓ Bill paying	70%
✓ Seeking career information	51%
✓ Completing job applications	41%
✓ Visiting library Web site	38%
✓ Applying for unemployment	28%
✓ Seeking public assistance information	21%

...compared to those not impacted.

✓ Social networking	64%
✓ Research	61%
✓ Banking	60%
✓ Bill paying	56%
✓ Visiting library Web site	32%
✓ Seeking career information	17%

or more of economically impacted Americans are doing research, banking and bill paying online compared to roughly 60% of those with no job impact.

As expected, the most significant differences in online activities between the economically impacted and nonimpacted are related to seeking career information (51% vs. 17%), completing job applications (41% vs. 12%), applying for unemployment (28% vs. 3%) and seeking public assistance information (21% vs. 7%).

Economically impacted Americans are also using the library more, both online and in person.

Economically impacted Americans are using the library more—and at greater rates

The differences in information consumption habits of Americans impacted by the economy extend to the use of information at the library. Those who have experienced a job impact are more likely to have a library card. Eighty-one percent (81%) of economically impacted Americans have a library card compared to 68% for Americans who have not been impacted.

Economically impacted Americans are 50% more likely to visit their library at least weekly (18% vs. 12%) and are nearly a third more likely to visit at least once a month (36% vs. 27%).

While at the library, those who have been economically impacted are more likely to use a broader range of services and are more likely to use those resources more frequently. Borrowing books and leisure reading are the top activities for all library users; but the economically impacted report a greater level of use, with a third borrowing books monthly. Borrowing DVDs and videos is an activity that 20% of economically impacted library users do monthly; twice the rate of those not impacted (11%).

Economically impacted Americans are making adjustments to their lifestyles and to their consumer-spending habits. The adjustments and how the library is filling the gap for these Americans is the focus of the next chapter.

THE LIBRARY...
EMPOWERING AMERICANS

The library empowers Americans with alternatives to spending

Americans are using libraries more in this challenging economic environment—a lot more.

To make ends meet, economically impacted Americans have reduced spending on leisure activities and entertainment, with the most substantial decreases in dining out and apparel. They buy fewer books, CDs and DVDs, and spend less on entertainment.

Library use fills the gap created by spending reductions.

More than a third (37%) of economically impacted respondents said they are using the library more often than they did before the economic downturn. Increased library use is substantially higher than any other lifestyle activity increase measured.

13 million economically impacted Americans—that is more than the populations of New York, Chicago and Houston combined—are using the library more during the challenging economic time.

One area where Americans have not cut back: cell phones and Internet access to stay connected. The majority did not change Internet, cable television, landline or mobile phone services. Americans will sacrifice other spending to stay connected.

Noneconomically impacted Americans use the library more, too. Sixteen percent (16%) of these respondents—or **23 million** nonimpacted Americans—cite an increase in library use. Library use is the lifestyle activity with the largest increase for all Americans.

We explore highlights from our data about Americans, economically impacted or not, who have increased their library use due to the economic environment.

ECONOMICALLY IMPACTED

Consumer spending has decreased.

76%

have reduced spending on books, CDs and DVDs.

The library fills the gap.

75%

who use the library more borrow books, CDs and DVDs instead of purchasing.

Library usage has increased.

ECONOMICALLY IMPACTED

Library use soars

Economically impacted Americans are using the library more—a lot more.

Library use

■ INCREASED   ■ DECREASED   ■ NO CHANGE   ■ NOT APPLICABLE

| INCREASED FOR 37% | 9% | 40% | 14% |

Economically impacted Americans are making lifestyle changes due to the economy

Americans are cutting back

| 5% | DECREASED FOR 86% | 7% | 2% |

Dining out

| 4% | DECREASED FOR 82% | 12% | 2% |

Apparel

| 5% | DECREASED FOR 80% | 11% | 3% |

Entertainment

| 4% | DECREASED FOR 76% | 16% | 3% |

Books, CDs, DVDs, etc.

| 5% | DECREASED FOR 74% | 13% | 8% |

Vacations

| 6% | DECREASED FOR 68% | 20% | 6% |

Electronics

| 5% | DECREASED FOR 53% | 26% | 15% |

Appliances

| 3% | DECREASED FOR 44% | 20% | 34% |

Memberships to clubs

| 5% | DECREASED FOR 42% | 46% | 7% |

Living quarters/space

Americans aren't saving as much

| 11% | DECREASED FOR 64% | 17% | 8% |

Savings/retirement

| 4% | DECREASED FOR 32% | 18% | 46% |

College education

Americans are staying connected

| 6% | 34% | NO CHANGE FOR 55% | 6% |

Mobile phone services

| 3% | 32% | NO CHANGE FOR 54% | 11% |

Landline phone

| 5% | 31% | NO CHANGE FOR 56% | 8% |

Cable television services

| 8% | 14% | NO CHANGE FOR 74% | 4% |

Internet service at home

The library empowers Americans with technology

Libraries provide access to technology for those hit hardest by the recession. More than half of economically impacted Americans who increased their library use—7 million—turn to the library more often to access technology. Free Internet and Wi-Fi access and computer use are particularly important. Economically impacted Americans use these library resources more often—at twice the rate of nonimpacted library users.

Economically impacted Americans who are using the library for computer and Internet access find real economic value in these offerings. Over half (63%) indicated they would not be likely to pay for computer/Internet access elsewhere if the library did not offer it. For most, it is their only alternative.

7 MILLION
economically impacted Americans have increased their use of technology at the library.

Technology at the library empowers

Americans who have increased their library use are...	ECONOMICALLY IMPACTED	NOT IMPACTED
Borrowing books, CDs, DVDs, etc., more often	91%	79%
Accessing the Internet for free more often	35%	14%
Reading magazines more often	29%	23%
Using the computer more often	28%	12%
Accessing the free Wi-Fi (wireless Internet) more often	24%	9%
Seeking public assistance information more often	24%	2%
Completing/submitting job applications more often	20%	0%
Seeking college-related information more often	19%	4%
Attending workshops/training classes more often	18%	6%
Helping family/friends find jobs more often	18%	2%

Economically impacted Americans are using the library to find jobs, and—for the first time— they are also...

- ☑ Using the computer

- ☑ Applying for local, state or federal aid (excluding unemployment)

- ☑ Attending a meeting/ community event

- ☑ Attending child-related events

- ☑ Attending professional/ career development/ training classes

- ☑ Seeking unemployment information

- ☑ Reading magazines

> ❝ I have two pretty [bad] jobs and can use some help from other sources to find a new job. The library is perfect for such a task.❞
>
> 47-YEAR-OLD, ECONOMICALLY IMPACTED AMERICAN

The library empowers Americans to revive careers

Libraries are vital in providing employment resources to the economically impacted. A third rely on library resources more often, or are using the library for the first time, for assistance in reviving careers. Career-related activities conducted at the library more frequently since the economic downturn include:

- Submitting job applications
- Seeking college-related information
- Seeking public assistance
- Helping family or friends find jobs
- Attending educational workshops.

The library is essential for job-related activities, such as seeking assistance in preparing a resume and for finding general job information, for a third (33%) of those who have experienced a job impact—or 4.4 million economically impacted Americans. Many library users also say that their library provides a place to think about their future and prepare for what is next.

Americans rely on their library for job-seeking activities. Fifty percent (50%) of the economically impacted using the library for job-related activities would not be likely to pay for these services elsewhere if the library did not provide them.

And, the library empowers beyond technology and careers

Economically impacted Americans are using the library more frequently for technology, careers and much more—discovering and using many of the more traditional resources for the first time. Economically impacted Americans are 50% more likely to visit the library weekly compared with those not impacted by the economy (18% vs. 12%). First-time library activities among the economically impacted include reading magazines, attending children's events and participating in community meetings.

HOW AMERICANS USE ONLINE SOURCES AND THEIR LIBRARIES

Online sources are heavily used but users are less impressed

Growth in the use of online sources including e-mail, search engines, social networking (e.g., Facebook), social media (e.g., YouTube) and ask-an-expert sites (e.g., Yahoo! Answers) has continued to climb since 2005, with search engines and e-mail hitting almost total saturation with online users. Economically impacted Americans are even greater users of online resources, especially social networking and media sites. Use of library online resources and the library Web site does not reflect the growth trend, with online library use levels flat to 2005.

As Americans become more familiar, maybe even expert, with a wide range of online services, excitement with and overall impressions of information resources have declined. Information consumers are just less impressed with information sources than they were five years ago.

E-mail and search engines hold on as top resources, but social sites are closing in fast

E-mail (94%) and search engines (92%) still lead as the most widely used online resources with usage rates for both services jumping up almost 30% when compared to our 2005 study results. Most use e-mail and search engines daily. Half of Americans report using e-mail alerts as a primary means of receiving news and information. E-mail and search engines have achieved near-ubiquitous status among online Americans, and social networking and social media are quickly catching up.

With 66% of Americans now using social sites, the reach of these sites has exploded in the last four years. Social sites were among the fastest growing online resources in our survey. More than half

All ages click here

Social use skyrockets

The popularity of social sites has **doubled** in the last three years. **All ages are participating.**

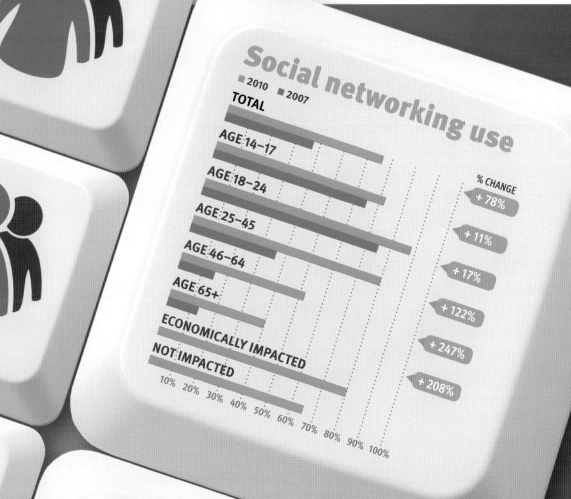

Social networking use

■ 2010 ■ 2007

% CHANGE

TOTAL	+ 78%
AGE 14–17	+ 11%
AGE 18–24	+ 17%
AGE 25–45	+ 122%
AGE 46–64	+ 247%
AGE 65+	+ 208%
ECONOMICALLY IMPACTED	
NOT IMPACTED	

10% 20% 30% 40% 50% 60% 70% 80% 90% 100%

Social media use

■ 2010 ■ 2007

% CHANGE

TOTAL	+ 106%
AGE 14–17	+ 55%
AGE 18–24	+ 52%
AGE 25–45	+ 143%
AGE 46–64	+ 241%
AGE 65+	+ 278%
ECONOMICALLY IMPACTED	
NOT IMPACTED	

10% 20% 30% 40% 50% 60% 70% 80% 90% 100%

of social networking users log on daily (55%), with 80% visiting at least once a week. While social media site use (e.g., YouTube, Flickr, etc.) led the use of social networking sites (e.g, MySpace, Facebook and LinkedIn, etc.) in 2007, the distinction between social media and networking sites has quickly blurred. Social media users now log on to these sites less often than social networking users do—15% daily and 47% weekly—but more of the traditional social networking sites now offer media and content exchange as part of the service.

Social sites were used predominantly by teens (ages 14–17) and young adults (ages 18–24) in 2007 when OCLC released the *Sharing, Privacy and Trust in Our Networked World* report. Since then, there has been triple-digit growth in the use of social sites among Americans age 25 and older. Americans ages 25–45 are now using social sites at rates similar to young adults, and even exceed teens in their use of social networking.

2010 survey results reveal that Americans who have experienced a negative job impact are using social networking sites at even higher rates than Americans not impacted (80% vs. 64%), and they are also more likely to use social media sites (71% vs. 66%).

No one started their information search on a library Web site

We asked information consumers in 2005 where they were most likely to start their search for information. Eighty-two percent (82%) reported that they began their information search on a search engine. One percent (1%) indicated that they started their search for information on a library Web site. When we surveyed information consumers in 2010, they were just as strongly tied to search engines as the starting point for information, with 84% beginning on a search engine. Not a single survey respondent began their information search on a library Web site.

While we did not inquire about the use of Wikipedia as a starting point for an information search in 2005, 3% of information seekers began their information searches on Wikipedia in 2010.

Where do Americans begin their information search?

Search engine
2005: **82%**
2010: **84%**

Wikipedia
2005: **NA**
2010: **3%**

Library Web site
2005: **1%**
2010: **0%**

Library Web site use

31% 2005   33% 2010

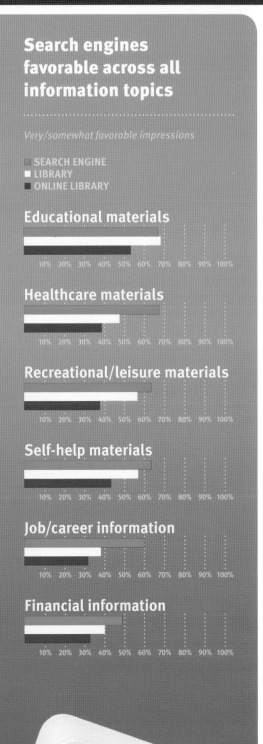

Search engines favorable across all information topics

Very/somewhat favorable impressions

■ SEARCH ENGINE
■ LIBRARY
■ ONLINE LIBRARY

Educational materials

10% 20% 30% 40% 50% 60% 70% 80% 90% 100%

Healthcare materials

10% 20% 30% 40% 50% 60% 70% 80% 90% 100%

Recreational/leisure materials

10% 20% 30% 40% 50% 60% 70% 80% 90% 100%

Self-help materials

10% 20% 30% 40% 50% 60% 70% 80% 90% 100%

Job/career information

10% 20% 30% 40% 50% 60% 70% 80% 90% 100%

Financial information

10% 20% 30% 40% 50% 60% 70% 80% 90% 100%

Although not the starting point for online information searches, library Web sites are used by a third of Americans.

Although not the starting point for online information searches, library Web sites are used by a third of Americans. Use of the library Web site has remained relatively steady (33% in 2010 from 31% in 2005). Use of online databases has also held steady, at about 16% in both 2005 and 2010.

We surveyed information consumers about their overall impressions of search engines, libraries and online libraries related to the availability of six types of information: educational materials, recreation/leisure materials, self-help materials, healthcare materials, financial/money management information and job/career information. Search engines garnered the highest favorability ratings for each except for educational materials, where libraries and search engines nearly tie. Despite the higher favorability ratings for search engines, information consumers recognized the critical role libraries play. Nearly half or more of Americans attribute favorable ratings to the library related to the availability of self-help materials (57%), recreation/leisure materials (57%) and healthcare materials (48%) at the library. Two-fifths view the library as favorable for financial/money management information (40%) and job/career information (38%).

Americans who experienced a negative job impact provide even higher favorability ratings for both search engines and libraries. Three-fourths view the library as favorable for educational materials (79%) and recreation/leisure materials (75%). More than half attribute favorable ratings to job/career information (51%), financial/money management information (51%), healthcare materials (60%) and self-help materials (68%) at the library. Search engines again were rated higher than libraries.

The use of ask-an-expert sites explodes

One of the most significant changes noted from the 2005 study was the marked increase in the use of online reference, or "ask-an-expert" services. Ask-an-expert sites (i.e., question & answer sites) have experienced a tremendous increase in use, nearly tripling since 2005. Today, 43% of information consumers report using an ask-an-expert site, up from just 15% in 2005.

Young adults showed the largest growth in demand, with use up 350%. Today, 40% of teens are monthly users of online "ask-an-expert" services.

Respondents indicated that they used online librarian question sites "as needed," but the popularity of ask-a-librarian sites has not seen the same spike in use as ask-an-expert sites. In fact, ask-a-librarian sites have increased only slightly since 2005 (5% to 7%) and remain relatively unused or undiscovered. Availability of ask-a-librarian sites has increased since 2005, with an estimated 58% of libraries now providing such services (ALA, June 2010).

Wikipedia now a staple, Skype and Twitter on the rise

Wikipedia is now used by 73% of Americans, with half of these users visiting the site at least once a month. This usage rate rivals both search engines and social sites, making Wikipedia an information staple for online Americans.

We asked about the use of two new social services that did not exist when we polled users in 2005: Skype and Twitter. Per Wikipedia, Skype is a software application that allows users to make voice and video calls over the Internet. In 2010, two in ten Americans (20%) indicated in our survey that they had used Skype. A recent version of the Skype software offers linking to Facebook.

Per Wikipedia, Twitter is a social networking and microblogging service that enables its users to send and read messages called "tweets", text-based posts of up to 140 characters that can be displayed on a user's profile page. It was launched in 2006. By early 2010, two in ten Americans we surveyed (18%) had used Twitter.

The most popular library activities still revolve around reading

The most popular activities among library users continue to be borrowing books and leisure reading. Two-fifths of these Americans go to the library at least annually for leisure reading

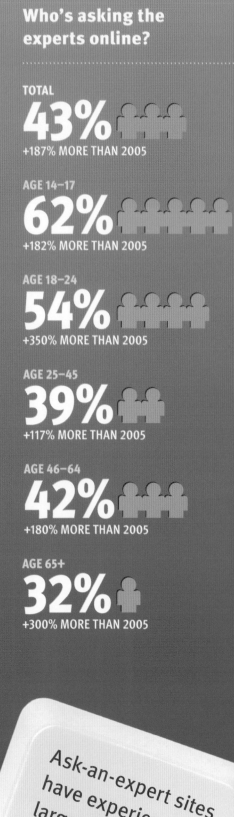

Who's asking the experts online?

TOTAL
43%
+187% MORE THAN 2005

AGE 14–17
62%
+182% MORE THAN 2005

AGE 18–24
54%
+350% MORE THAN 2005

AGE 25–45
39%
+117% MORE THAN 2005

AGE 46–64
42%
+180% MORE THAN 2005

AGE 65+
32%
+300% MORE THAN 2005

Ask-an-expert sites have experienced large gains in use, nearly tripling since 2005—from 15 to 43 percent.

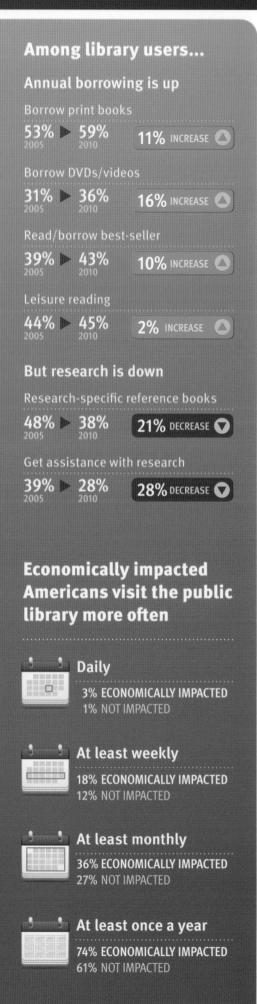

Among library users...

Annual borrowing is up

Borrow print books

53% ▶ 59%   11% INCREASE ▲
2005   2010

Borrow DVDs/videos

31% ▶ 36%   16% INCREASE ▲
2005   2010

Read/borrow best-seller

39% ▶ 43%   10% INCREASE ▲
2005   2010

Leisure reading

44% ▶ 45%   2% INCREASE ▲
2005   2010

But research is down

Research-specific reference books

48% ▶ 38%   21% DECREASE ▼
2005   2010

Get assistance with research

39% ▶ 28%   28% DECREASE ▼
2005   2010

Economically impacted Americans visit the public library more often

Daily

3% ECONOMICALLY IMPACTED
1% NOT IMPACTED

At least weekly

18% ECONOMICALLY IMPACTED
12% NOT IMPACTED

At least monthly

36% ECONOMICALLY IMPACTED
27% NOT IMPACTED

At least once a year

74% ECONOMICALLY IMPACTED
61% NOT IMPACTED

(45%). Borrowing books continues to hold the top spot with 28% of Americans borrowing print books monthly and 59% borrowing books at least once a year.

A significant number of Americans are borrowing books even more often—a 23% bump in monthly borrowers and 11% increase in annual borrowers. Two in ten Americans also come to the library annually to read magazines (27%) and newspapers (19%).

Beyond reading, borrowing DVDs/videos also increased. A third of Americans (36%) borrow DVDs/videos annually. A quarter of Americans use technology provided by the library, such as computers (27%) and Internet (28%), at least once a year.

Library services are used even more by Americans impacted by the recession. Americans impacted by job loss are using the library at greater rates and are using a full range of library services, in addition to reading. Twice as many economically impacted Americans regularly borrow DVDs/videos (20% vs. 11% monthly). More than a third of economically impacted Americans use the computers (35%) and access the Internet for free (35%) annually at the library.

Research activity is down. Fewer Americans report conducting research activities at the library compared to five years ago. While over a third of Americans continue to conduct research at the library at least once a year, use of library research services has declined. Use of reference books is down 21% from 2005, now at 38%. Fewer Americans are asking for assistance with research at the library; 28% of users ask for help annually compared to 39% annually in 2005, a decrease of 28%.

While information resource use grows, overall impressions decline

Americans are just not as impressed with their information resources as they were in 2005. While almost all information resources saw marked increases in use over 2005, favorability rating of both online and offline information resources have declined since 2005. Favorable ratings have declined for search engines, physical libraries, online bookstores and physical bookstores. Social networking and social media sites were not in use and therefore not rated in 2005, so perception shifts are not available.

In 2005 the majority of Americans assigned strong favorability ratings to many information resources. Search engines topped the list with an 86% favorability rating. That rating has dropped 12 points to 74% in 2010.

Libraries (80%) and bookstores (78%) also earned high, and similar, favorability ratings in 2005. Both resources have slipped over 10 points in favorability in 2010, but remain similar with a favorability rating at 66% for libraries and 65% for bookstores.

Favorability ratings of the online library remain steady from 2005, at 45%.

Our findings suggest that as online resources become more commonplace, the shine has likely dulled. Information consumers

MORE THAN
10-POINT
DROP IN FAVORABILITY FOR
INFORMATION SOURCES
Online bookstores
Physical bookstores
Search engines
Physical libraries

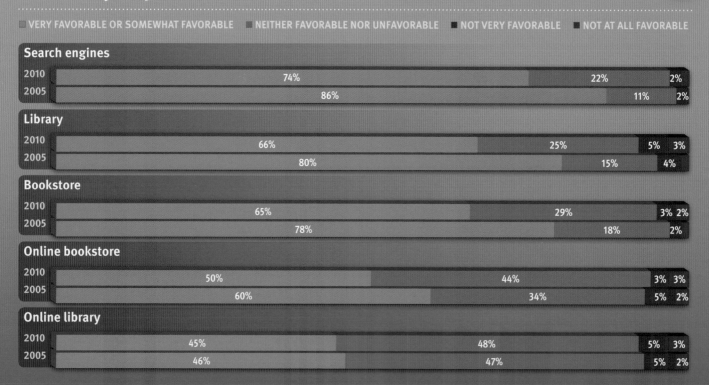

Favorability drops for all information sources

■ VERY FAVORABLE OR SOMEWHAT FAVORABLE   ■ NEITHER FAVORABLE NOR UNFAVORABLE   ■ NOT VERY FAVORABLE   ■ NOT AT ALL FAVORABLE

Search engines

2010	74%	22%	2%
2005	86%	11%	2%

Library

2010	66%	25%	5%	3%
2005	80%	15%	4%	

Bookstore

2010	65%	29%	3%	2%
2005	78%	18%	2%	

Online bookstore

2010	50%	44%	3%	3%
2005	60%	34%	5%	2%

Online library

2010	45%	48%	5%	3%
2005	46%	47%	5%	2%

are also likely to increase their expectations of all online resources as more features are added and new and more alternatives are introduced. And finally, the impact of the struggling U.S. economic environment is likely another factor lowering overall optimism and favorability.

Users' 2005 expectations about future library use prove accurate

Information consumers surveyed in 2005 accurately predicted their future library use. The majority (61%) predicted that their library use would remain steady in the next three to five years. The 2010 survey results reveal that half of users (52%) indicated their library use had remained the same in the previous year. Almost a quarter (21%) of 2005 respondents thought they would increase their library use and, indeed, a similar proportion of 2010 information consumers reported growth (27%).

Top reasons cited for increases in library use are:

- To save money (borrowing instead of purchasing) (75%)
- My children enjoy visiting the library (27%)
- Homework/school demands (25%)
- More available time (25%).

Information consumers also accurately predicted decreases in library use. Eighteen percent (18%) of Americans predicted that their library use would decline. Twenty-one percent (21%) of 2010 respondents reported a drop in library use.

The top reasons for decreased library use include:

- Less available time (33%)
- No need since leaving school/college (28%)
- Unable to get to library because homebound or disabled (20%)
- Prefer to purchase materials (16%)
- Library has an outdated collection (13%).

THE LIBRARY BRAND 2010

The library brand—it's still BOOKS

The library brand is "books." "Libraries = books" is even stronger than it was five years ago. As new consumer devices and online services have captured the information consumer's time and mindshare, his perception of libraries as books has solidified.

In 2005, most Americans (69%) said "books" is the first thing that comes to mind when thinking about the library. In 2010, even more, 75%, believe that the library brand is books.

While the battle of e-resources and services has intensified across an increasing number of providers and services over the last five years, the landscape of print book suppliers for consumers has remained largely the same—Amazon, a few other large book suppliers and libraries. Earlier we reviewed the number-one activity at U.S. libraries is "borrowing print books," followed by "leisure reading." When respondents were asked to identify the most important role of the library, "books, videos and music" topped the list. This view was consistent across all age groups surveyed with the exception of teens ages 14–17, who indicated that "a place to read" was the most important library role to them. Libraries as a source of books remain both top-of-mind and top-of-personal-value for Americans.

Will the books brand perception shift as libraries increase their investments and advertising in electronic information and electronic books? A shift in expenditures from predominantly print, to print and electronic, is clearly underway. Public libraries increased expenditures on e-resources by 66% from 2003 to 2008, according to the Institute of Museum and Library Services. During this same time period, academic libraries increased e-resource expenditures by 233%, according to National Center for Education Statistics. *USA Today* reported in January 2011 that sales of the

Even more Americans associate libraries with books.

75%
IN 2010

69%
IN 2005

What is the first thing you think of when you think of the library?

Books

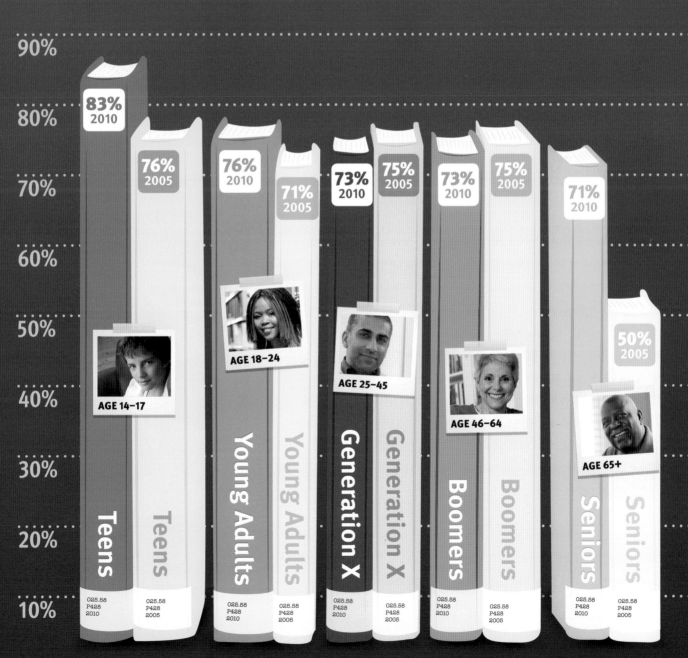

83% 2010 — Teens (AGE 14–17)
025.58 P428 2010

76% 2005 — Teens
025.58 P428 2005

76% 2010 — Young Adults (AGE 18–24)
025.58 P428 2010

71% 2005 — Young Adults
025.58 P428 2005

73% 2010 — Generation X (AGE 25–45)
025.58 P428 2010

75% 2005 — Generation X
025.58 P428 2005

73% 2010 — Boomers (AGE 46–64)
025.58 P428 2010

75% 2005 — Boomers
025.58 P428 2005

71% 2010 — Seniors (AGE 65+)
025.58 P428 2010

50% 2005 — Seniors
025.58 P428 2005

90% 80% 70% 60% 50% 40% 30% 20% 10%

e-book versions of the top six best-seller books from the last week of December 2010 exceeded print for the first time. Changing perceptions of libraries from books to another role would require both awareness and widespread use of electronic information services. In our 2005 study, we found that most Americans were not aware their library provided e-resources. This low level of awareness of e-resources was evident again in our 2010 study. Most information consumers continue to be unaware their library has online databases (56%), e-books (56%) and e-journals (60%).

As we did in the 2005 study, we asked not only about the "top of mind" associations with the library but also about the overall purpose of libraries. The belief that the main purpose of the library is to "provide information" remains the top belief for Americans. Half of respondents mentioned "information" as the library's main purpose, followed by a third who said the top purpose of the library is to "provide books." Perceptions of both the brand and the purpose of the library remain unchanged from 2005.

Americans trust themselves, search engines and libraries

When comparing libraries to search engines, overwhelmingly, Americans consider search engines to be more convenient, faster, more reliable and easier-to-use. Americans consider libraries to be more trustworthy and more accurate.

While Americans ranked libraries ahead of search engines in trustworthiness and accuracy, this distinction evaporates when asked about the **information** that is provided by search engines and libraries. Most Americans (69%) believe the information they find using search engines is just as trustworthy as they would find from their library. This perception was well-established in 2005 and remains as strong in 2010.

Information consumers are self-confident and want to self-serve. When asked how they select information sources, they say they look for a source that provides worthwhile, trustworthy and free information. Ease of use and speed are important criteria, but not

---

Libraries vs. search engines

Libraries: more trustworthy

Libraries (online or physical) are considered:

More trustworthy	🏛 65%	🔍 35%
More accurate	🏛 58%	🔍 42%

Search engines: faster

Search engines are considered:

Faster	🔍 91%	🏛 9%
More convenient	🔍 90%	🏛 10%
Easier-to-use	🔍 83%	🏛 17%
More reliable	🔍 72%	🏛 28%

Information from library sources is...

About the same 69%
Less trustworthy 5%
More trustworthy 26%

2010

About the same 70%
Less trustworthy 9%
More trustworthy 21%

2005

...compared to search engines.

How do Americans choose an information source?

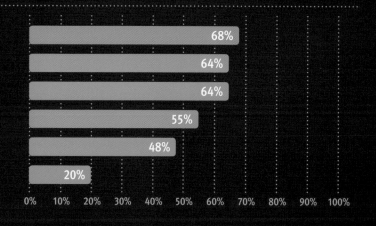

Worthwhile information	68%
Trustworthy information	64%
Free information	64%
Ease of use	55%
Fast information	48%
Based on a recommendation	20%

How do we know it's trustworthy?

Information consumers rely on themselves to determine the trustworthiness of information.

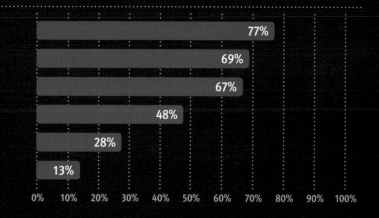

Based on personal knowledge/common sense	77%
Cross-referencing with other sites or sources	69%
Based on the reputation of the company/organization	67%
Recommendation from a trusted source	48%
Based on the author/creator	28%
Based on the site's appearance	13%

Who or what is our trusted source?

22%	Search engine
16%	Expert in the field of interest
13%	Other Web sites with similar information
10%	Friend
6%	Library materials
3%	Wikipedia
1%	Librarian

the top factors. When it comes to judging the trustworthiness of the information, information consumers "just know." They use personal knowledge and common sense. If they are in doubt, they will cross-reference with other sites or sources.

Judging the trustworthiness of information based on recommendations from a trusted source continues to be important for about half (48%) of information seekers, but down from 2005 (55%). Information consumers' top trusted source is the search engine (22%). Information consumers trust themselves, search engines and libraries for information.

We asked about Wikipedia for the first time in 2010. Americans use Wikipedia (73%) with use rates nearing those of search engines (92%). While used extensively, Wikipedia is not seen as trustworthy as libraries. The majority (51%) rate information from library sources as more trustworthy than from Wikipedia.

Americans appreciate and value librarians

Americans see and appreciate the value of librarians. The vast majority (83%) of Americans who have used a librarian agree librarians add value to the search process, even more so than in 2005 (76%). Respondents who had experienced a negative job impact rate librarians even higher, with 88% indicating the librarian adds value to the search process.

Information consumers continue to be highly satisfied with the library and librarian experience. Survey results show a growth in the number of respondents who agree libraries provide the personnel, technology, information resources and physical environment that meet their needs. In fact, we see a 25% increase in those who indicated that they are very satisfied with the overall search experience with the librarian.

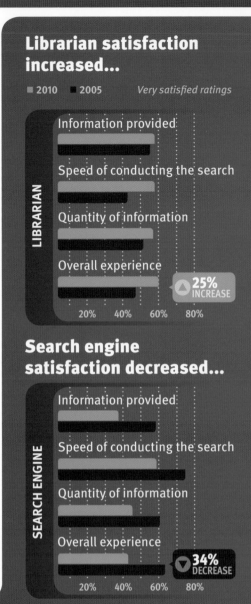

Librarian satisfaction increased...

■ 2010 ■ 2005   *Very satisfied ratings*

LIBRARIAN

Information provided

Speed of conducting the search

Quantity of information

Overall experience

▲ **25% INCREASE**

20% 40% 60% 80%

Search engine satisfaction decreased...

SEARCH ENGINE

Information provided

Speed of conducting the search

Quantity of information

Overall experience

▼ **34% DECREASE**

20% 40% 60% 80%

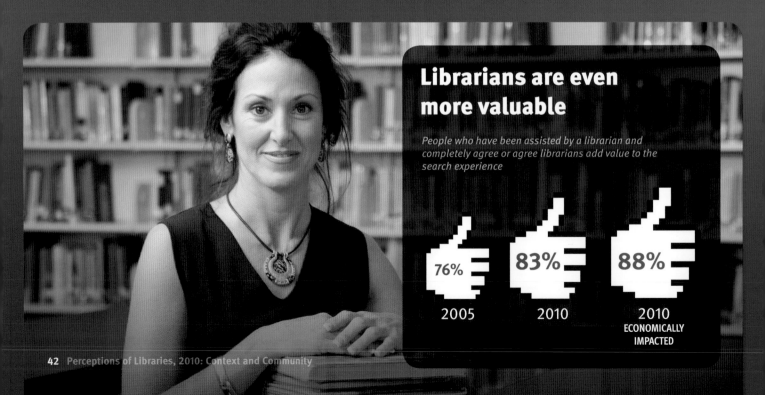

Librarians are even more valuable

People who have been assisted by a librarian and completely agree or agree librarians add value to the search experience

76% 2005

83% 2010

88% 2010 ECONOMICALLY IMPACTED

84% of total respondents begin their search for information using a search engine;
no respondents begin at the library Web site.

As the ratings of the librarian's value in the search process climbed, the satisfaction with the experience when using a search engine declined. In the last five years, search engines have seen a 34% decline in very satisfied ratings for overall experience, with 41% indicating in 2010 that they are very satisfied, down from 62% in 2005.

Why don't you use the library Web site?

 39% I didn't know it existed.

 28% I prefer to use the library in person.

 10% I don't have a library card.

10% Other Web sites have better information.

The belief that librarians add value in the search process has not transferred to the online library. As noted earlier in the report, the use of the library Web site remained flat from 2005 and no respondents started their search for information on the library Web site. The information consumer starts her information search on search engines. Fourteen percent (14%) of searchers who started on a search engine ended up at the library Web site. The majority who arrived at the library Web site used it, and with good results. Most (80%) found what they needed and over half have returned to use the site.

Much work remains to connect information consumers with library resources, but those who find the library Web site find success.

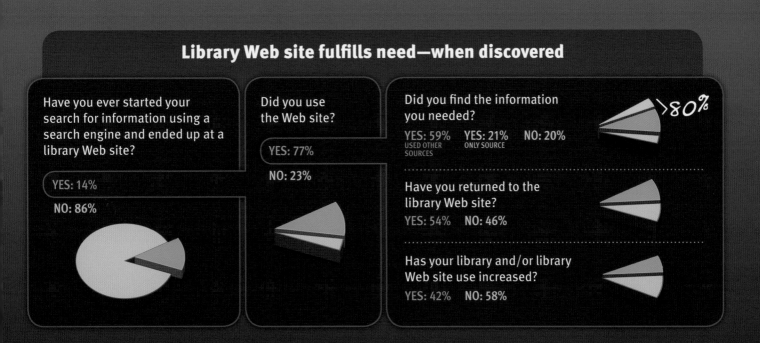

Library Web site fulfills need—when discovered

Have you ever started your search for information using a search engine and ended up at a library Web site?

YES: 14%

NO: 86%

Did you use the Web site?

YES: 77%

NO: 23%

Did you find the information you needed?

YES: 59% USED OTHER SOURCES   YES: 21% ONLY SOURCE   NO: 20%

>80%

Have you returned to the library Web site?

YES: 54%   NO: 46%

Has your library and/or library Web site use increased?

YES: 42%   NO: 58%

Americans believe the library has become more valuable to their communities due to the recession. Not only have Americans increased their use of the library, but they have an increased belief that the library is an important community asset. A third of all Americans (31%)—or 60 million Americans age 14 and over—see an increase in the value of the library for their communities. And, for Americans who have had a negative job impact, the increased value of the library is an even greater percentage (40%)—or equal to over 14 million economically impacted Americans.

Our study shows that the library continues to be used, and perceived, as an important source of books and other materials, both for information consumers and their communities. And the 2010 report also highlights the belief that the library is an increasingly important community asset as a place that provides the ability to save money in tough economic times, as a place to learn and read, and as a place to support literacy in America.

Americans see increased value of the library

Americans believe the library is a socially valued institution. Our survey asked respondents to indicate how the value of the library has changed for them, their families or their communities during the recent recession. We also asked the information consumers to share what they believe is the most important role of the library for themselves personally and for their communities.

Millions of Americans, across all age groups, indicated that the value of the library has increased during the recent recession. Information consumers believe the value has increased even more for their communities (31%) than for themselves (21%) or families (19%). Each age group has double-digit percentages that see an increased value of the libraries for themselves as well as an increased value for their families and their communities. College

> **"** The library continues to allow access to training and education to all who seek it regardless of ability to pay. **The public library system saves lives, careers and futures."**
>
> **61-YEAR-OLD ECONOMICALLY IMPACTED**

Value of the library has increased for...

% of respondents

ME

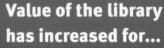

135% Difference

MY COMMUNITY

38% Difference

MY FAMILY

127% Difference

10%   20%   30%   40%

■ ECONOMICALLY IMPACTED
■ NOT IMPACTED
■ TOTAL U.S. RESPONDENTS

Libraries...valuable to the community

Americans' perceived value of the library has increased for themselves personally—**and even more so for their community.**

The value of the library has... *% of respondents*

COLLEGE STUDENTS

32%
INCREASED
FOR ME

31%
INCREASED
FOR MY COMMUNITY

AGE 14–17

19%
INCREASED
FOR ME

21%
INCREASED
FOR MY COMMUNITY

AGE 18–24

27%
INCREASED
FOR ME

26%
INCREASED
FOR MY COMMUNITY

AGE 25–45

25%
INCREASED
FOR ME

33%
INCREASED
FOR MY COMMUNITY

AGE 46–64

18%
INCREASED
FOR ME

30%
INCREASED
FOR MY COMMUNITY

AGE 65+

16%
INCREASED
FOR ME

36%
INCREASED
FOR MY COMMUNITY

students agree. A third of all college students see an increase in the value of the library for themselves, as well as for their communities, during the recent recession.

The age groups that see the largest personal increase in value are Americans between ages 18 and 45. A quarter of these Americans believe the library is more valuable today than it was before the recession. For college students, the personal value was even greater, at 32%.

Our study found that older Americans were more likely to indicate an increased value of the library for the community. While 21% of teens (ages 14–17) indicated that the value of the library had increased for their community, more than a third (36%) of seniors (age 65 and older) see an increase in value to their community.

Economically impacted Americans are most likely to see increased library value, with 40% indicating that the value has increased both for them personally and for their communities, and 34% indicating increased value for their families. When compared to those not impacted, economically impacted Americans are twice as likely to recognize increased value for themselves and their families, and 38% more likely for their communities.

Americans who have not experienced a negative job impact due to the recession are more likely to indicate an increased library value for their communities rather than for themselves. Almost a third (29%) of Americans not impacted cite a belief that library value has increased for their community as a result of the current economic environment, whereas 17% of them indicate increased library value on a personal level.

Not all Americans saw an increase in personal value of the library. Roughly 20% of Americans reported a decrease in personal value. The reasons included: finding information online is more convenient, libraries have had to reduce their hours or close and are not available when needed, and spending money on gas to get to the library is a challenge. Fewer economically impacted Americans reported a decline in personal value of the library, just 13%.

Library value has increased...

“ I can read lots of books for free instead of spending $10 for two hours of entertainment”

19-YEAR-OLD ECONOMICALLY IMPACTED COLLEGE STUDENT

“ They have gone out of their way to be sure everyone has access to what they need.”

74-YEAR-OLD

“ It has become a space I can use instead of going to a place where I would have to pay for internet or book services.”

23-YEAR-OLD ECONOMICALLY IMPACTED

Library value has decreased…

66 I read a lot but the library is not receiving funds to purchase new books that I would like to read."

49-YEAR-OLD

66 a library is starting to be in the past due to new technology allowing us to do the same things without actually going to a library"

16-YEAR-OLD

66 The computer has decreased my need to reference things at the library. I also belong to 2 book swaps online."

71-YEAR-OLD

Important library roles

Books, videos, music...most important to Americans and their communities

	What's most important to me?	What's most important to my community?
TOTAL U.S. RESPONDENTS	51% Books, videos and music 32% Makes needed information freely available	30% Books, videos and music 25% Supports literacy 24% Free Internet access
ECONOMICALLY IMPACTED	48% Books, videos and music 34% A place to read	30% Free information support to the less fortunate 28% Supports literacy
COLLEGE STUDENTS	35% Books, videos and music 32% Place to learn	27% Books, videos and music 25% Supports literacy
AGE 14–17	33% Place to read 32% Books, videos and music	31% Free Internet access 23% Free computer use
AGE 18–24	36% Books, videos and music 31% Place to learn	30% Books, videos and music 27% Free Internet access
AGE 25–45	50% Books, videos and music 36% Makes needed information freely available	30% Books, videos and music 30% Free information support to the less fortunate
AGE 46–64	60% Books, videos and music 31% A place to read	31% Books, videos and music 28% Supports literacy
AGE 65+	60% Books, videos and music 42% Makes needed information freely available	34% Books, videos and music 24% Supports literacy

Overwhelmingly, Americans view the library's role as a place to get **books, videos and music**.

Books, videos and music are as important to them **personally** as this role is to their **communities**.

The most important role of the library: a place for books, videos and music

Overwhelmingly, Americans view the library's role as a place to get books, videos and music, a role that is as important to them personally as to their community. A place to learn, read and to make information freely available are library roles Americans feel are more important to them personally than for their community. Meanwhile, free Internet and computer access, supporting literacy and providing information support to the less fortunate are library roles more important to their communities.

There is consistency across most age groups that a place to get books, videos and music is the most important role the library plays personally. Teens are the exception. The most important role the library plays for those ages 14–17 personally is as a place to read.

Most Americans feel the most important role the library plays for the community is a place for books, videos and music. Teens view the most important library role for the community differently. Teens feel free Internet access is the top library role for the community.

For those Americans who have been economically impacted, the most important role the library plays for them personally is the same as it is for almost all Americans—as a place to get books, videos and music. When it comes to the community, though, the economically impacted see the library's most important role as a provider of free information support to the less fortunate.

College students feel the most important library role for them personally and for their community is a place for books, videos and music. A place to learn is the second most important role to college students personally, while supporting literacy is the second most important role for their community.

By Community

The 2005 study was our first view into how the use of information resources, technology and libraries varied by age. Five years later, we wanted to understand more about how different user communities use and perceive online resources and their libraries—what was different, what activities and beliefs were shared, and if the lines between the generations and online activities were blurring, or becoming more defined, as technologies evolved.

As in 2005, teens (ages 14–17), young adults (ages 18–24) and college students adopt new technologies quickly. Today, teens lead in the use of ask-an-expert sites. Young adults and college students are the most active social networking and media users. Gen Xers (ages 25–45), Boomers (ages 46–64) and Seniors (age 65+) are closing the gap with triple-digit growth over the last three years in social site use.

Americans, no matter their life stage, are relying more heavily on libraries during tough economic times. The economic downturn had the most negative job impact on Gen Xers and Boomers, who are most likely to have reduced spending on entertainment, books, CDs, DVDs and dining out—and to have increased their library use.

Perceptions and online resource use varied fairly widely across age groups and between students and nonstudents, but the gaps from 2005 are closing. The beliefs and attitudes about libraries and librarians were strikingly similar across age groups, but library use varied widely.

We wanted to capture their views and advice to libraries in information consumers' own words. A summary of their advice and sample quotes are provided for each community. Teens, young adults, Gen Xers and college students advise the library to update and add to their collections, while Boomers and Seniors advise the library to extend hours.

The library offers valued service across all generations. The following is what we learned.

COLLEGE STUDENTS

AGE 14–17

AGE 18–24

AGE 25–45

AGE 46–64

AGE 65+

College students continue to adopt new online services

Use of online information sources increased for college students since 2005. Use of most sources continues to be higher among college students compared to U.S. total respondents. College students have quickly adopted new resources, such as Skype and Twitter.

E-mail use has hit saturation—99% of college students use e-mail and most e-mail daily. E-mail has its rivals. Fast adoption of social networking and media has placed sites such as Facebook and YouTube at the top of most-used online sources—going from almost nonexistent to ubiquitous in less than four years. Most (92%) college students use social networking sites; 81% use social media sites. Two-thirds of students who use social networking log on daily.

Search engines continue to dominate, topping the list of electronic sources most used to find online content (93%), followed closely by Wikipedia (88%). The key difference in usage between search engines and Wikipedia is the frequency—75% of students who use search engines do so daily, compared to 20% of those who use Wikipedia.

Results show a decline in use of library Web sites, electronic journals and online databases since 2005. This drop is driven by a decrease in use among college students ages 25–64. Use rates among 18–24-year-old students show a modest increase for library Web sites (53% to 58%), while e-journal use declined slightly (41% vs. 39%) and online database use did not change (30%). While the number of college students using the library Web site declined (61% to 57%), those who do so are using it more frequently—22% use it at least weekly, up from 15% in 2005.

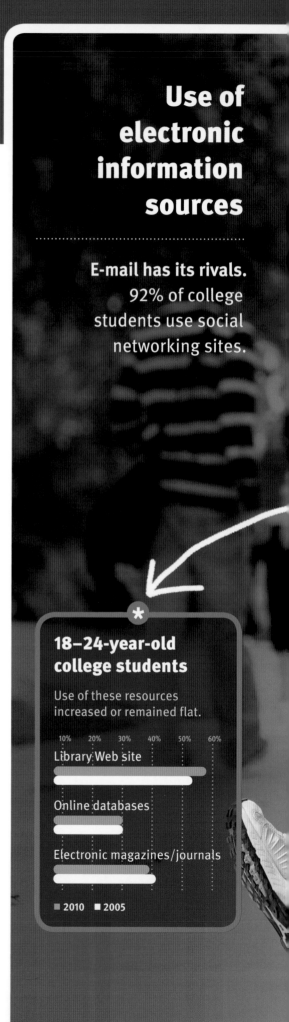

Use of electronic information sources

E-mail has its rivals.
92% of college students use social networking sites.

*
18–24-year-old college students

Use of these resources increased or remained flat.

10% 20% 30% 40% 50% 60%

Library Web site

Online databases

Electronic magazines/journals

■ 2010 ■ 2005

Social communication

0% 10% 20% 30% 40% 50% 60% 70% 80% 90% 100%

- 2010
- 2007
- 2005

E-mail

Instant messaging

Blogs

Social networking sites

Social media sites

Skype

Twitter

Finding content

0% 10% 20% 30% 40% 50% 60% 70% 80% 90% 100%

Search engines

Wikipedia

Online bookstores

Online news

Library Web site*

Electronic magazines/journals*

Online databases*

Getting answers

0% 10% 20% 30% 40% 50% 60% 70% 80% 90%

Ask-an-expert sites

Online librarian question service

Ask-an-expert sites (e.g., WikiAnswers) showed the largest five-year growth—136% increase. The frequency of use increased as well. The majority of college students who used these sites did so on an as-needed basis in 2005; now 30% search for answers at least monthly. College students are asking experts for help; are they asking librarians? Our survey results indicate that only a few are using online librarian question services—10% in 2010 vs. 8% in 2005. The number of academic libraries offering online reference services increased more than 10% from 2004 to 2008 (NCES).

Faster and easier trump trustworthy and accurate

College students overwhelmingly (83%) begin their information searches using search engines, though at lower rates than in 2005 (92%). As in 2005, no student surveyed started on the library Web site. College students feel that search engines trump libraries for speed, convenience, reliability and ease of use. Libraries trump search engines for trustworthiness and accuracy. Substantially more students in 2010 (43%) indicated that information from library sources is more trustworthy than from search engines (31% in 2005).

Where college students begin their information search

Search engine	83%
Wikipedia	7%
Social networking site	2%
E-mail	1%
E-mail subscription/alert	1%
Online database	1%
Ask-an-expert site	0%
Library Web site	0%
Online bookstore	0%
Topic-specific Web site	0%

Librarians are even more valuable than in 2005

College students who have been assisted by a librarian and who completely agree or agree librarians add value to the search process

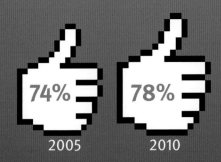

74%   78%

2005   2010

Information from library sources is...

■ 2010 ■ 2005

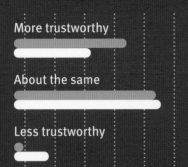

More trustworthy

About the same

Less trustworthy

10% 20% 30% 40% 50% 60%

...compared to search engines.

> **"** I realize how much valuable information [the library] has."
>
> **18-YEAR-OLD UNDERGRADUATE**

Information from library sources is...

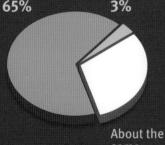

More trustworthy
65%

Less trustworthy
3%

About the same
30%

...compared to Wikipedia.

We asked students about the trustworthiness of Wikipedia for the first time. The majority (65%) believe that Wikipedia is less trustworthy than libraries, while 30% believe both are equally trustworthy.

Students determine which sources to use based on credibility and trustworthiness of information, if it is free and if it provides what they need. Fewer, about half, say they rely on ease of use and speed. Most students continue to rely on personal knowledge and common sense (78%) to determine the trustworthiness; this was among the top determinants in 2005. If college students question sources, they cross-reference with other Web sites or sources.

Trustworthiness and accuracy are cited as the most critical criteria for determining which information sources to use. However, behavior indicates that speed and convenience, and a strong belief that personal knowledge and common sense can determine credibility, continue to drive most search activity through nonlibrary resources. Eighty-eight percent (88%) of students use Wikipedia and 93% use search engines for finding online information. Just over half use the library Web site (57%).

Libraries: more trustworthy

Libraries (online or physical) are considered:

More trustworthy	76%	24%
More accurate	69%	31%

Search engines: faster

Search engines are considered:

Faster	92%	8%
More convenient	87%	13%
Easier to use	84%	16%
More reliable	64%	36%

Finding success at the library

While it may not be the first source college students turn to for information searching, the library is cited as an important information source by the majority. When cross-referencing information sources, more than half (56%) use library materials and 24% use a librarian. These rates are similar to 2005 results (57% and 29%).

Among college students who use a recommendation from a trusted source to determine the trustworthiness of information, 11% use library materials and 5% consult librarians. These rates are higher than in 2005 (5% and 2%).

College students recognize the value-add librarians provide to the search process. Three-quarters (78%) who use librarians agree librarians add value to the process and that librarian assistance is available when needed (71%). More college students are very satisfied with information, service and overall experience with librarians than they are with search engines, at rates roughly the same as in 2005.

Why don't college students use the library Web site?

23% Other sites have better information.

21% Prefer to use the library.

17% Web site does not have what I need.

12% Fines are too much.

11% Can't find what I need.

10% Did not know it existed.

Search engine satisfaction drops dramatically

■ 2010 ■ 2005

Very satisfied ratings

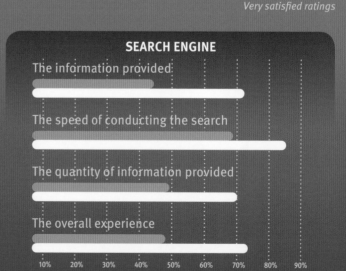

LIBRARIANS

The information provided

The speed of conducting the search

The quantity of information provided

The overall experience

10% 20% 30% 40% 50% 60% 70% 80% 90%

SEARCH ENGINE

The information provided

The speed of conducting the search

The quantity of information provided

The overall experience

10% 20% 30% 40% 50% 60% 70% 80% 90%

How has the library's value increased for you?

> **"** More valuable to use the libraries 'free' resources as way to cut back on my discretionary spending."
>
> 27-YEAR-OLD GRADUATE STUDENT

> **"** It's a hotspot for information and we live in an age of information so its the place to be."
>
> 18-YEAR-OLD UNDERGRADUATE

> **"** Since checking out books from the library is free it is a great value when money is tight. Free entertainment can't be beat."
>
> 25-YEAR-OLD ECONOMICALLY IMPACTED GRADUATE STUDENT

Library Web site fulfills need—when discovered

Most students begin their information search using a search engine, and 27% indicated they have started with a search engine and ended up at a library Web site. Of those who connect to the library Web site, most use the site (80%) and almost all who do so get to success (99%). About a third of students (34%) say that the library Web site was the only site used; two-thirds also used other sources (65%). Most who started at a search engine and ended up at a library Web site say they have returned to the site (69%), and 50% have increased their use of the library and/or library Web site.

Students who use the library Web site find success. However, over 40% of students indicate they have not used their library Web site, a rate similar to 2005. The top reason for not using the library Web site is not lack of awareness. Just 10% of students who do not use the library site indicated that they were not aware that it existed. The top reason for lack of use is the perception that other sites have better information (23%). This perception remains consistent with 2005 findings.

Library Web site fulfills need—when discovered

Have you ever started your search for information using a search engine and ended up at a library Web site?

YES: 27%

NO: 73%

Did you use the Web site?

YES: 80%

NO: 20%

Did you find the information you needed?

YES: 65% USED OTHER SOURCES   YES: 34% ONLY SOURCE   NO: 1%

>99%

Have you returned to the library Web site?

YES: 69%   NO: 31%

Has your library and/or library Web site use increased?

YES: 50%   NO: 50%

The value of the library has increased to college students

College students value the library. Appreciation for the library came through in both the data and open-ended statements. The value of the library was more apparent to many during the down economy. A third (32%) of students indicated that the library's value has increased for them personally during the recession, higher than for total U.S. respondents. College students also recognize the value for their community. A third (31%) believe that the library's value has increased for their community during the recession, a rate equal to the total U.S. respondents.

Important library roles for college students

What's most important to me?

35% Books, videos and music
32% Place to learn

What's most important to my community?

27% Books, videos and music
25% Support literacy

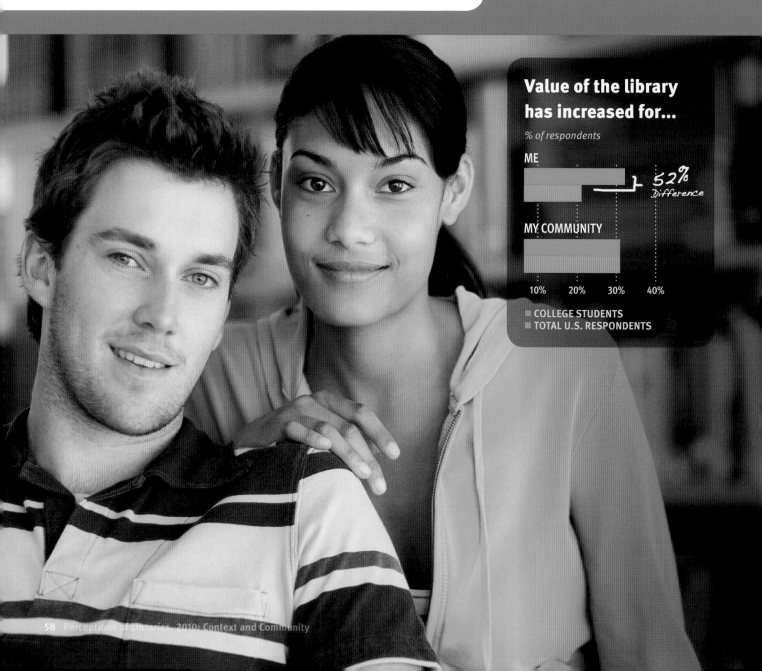

Value of the library has increased for...

% of respondents

ME

52% Difference

MY COMMUNITY

10% 20% 30% 40%

■ COLLEGE STUDENTS
■ TOTAL U.S. RESPONDENTS

Library activities down

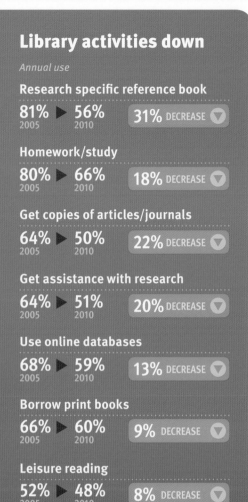

Annual use

Research specific reference book

81% ▶ 56%
2005   2010   **31% DECREASE** ▼

Homework/study

80% ▶ 66%
2005   2010   **18% DECREASE** ▼

Get copies of articles/journals

64% ▶ 50%
2005   2010   **22% DECREASE** ▼

Get assistance with research

64% ▶ 51%
2005   2010   **20% DECREASE** ▼

Use online databases

68% ▶ 59%
2005   2010   **13% DECREASE** ▼

Borrow print books

66% ▶ 60%
2005   2010   **9% DECREASE** ▼

Leisure reading

52% ▶ 48%
2005   2010   **8% DECREASE** ▼

When students identified the most important library role, the top response was "to provide books, videos and music"; "a place to learn" ranked second. These values mirror the top student library activities. The top 2010 annual library activities were homework/ study (66%) and borrow print books (60%). While library use trended down from 2005 across all resources, borrowing print books and leisure reading stayed relatively stable.

Students are less impressed with all online resources

Mirroring attitudes of nonstudents, college students had lower overall impressions of information resources than in 2005. Search engines had an 88% favorability rating in 2005, dropping to 70% in 2010. Likewise, favorability ratings dropped for libraries and bookstores, including online libraries and bookstores. Bookstores, online bookstores and online libraries have dropped to more neutral ratings. The physical library, like search engines, saw an 18-point slide from 2005.

Favorability drops for all information sources

■ VERY FAVORABLE OR SOMEWHAT FAVORABLE   ■ NEITHER FAVORABLE NOR UNFAVORABLE   ■ NOT VERY FAVORABLE   ■ NOT AT ALL FAVORABLE

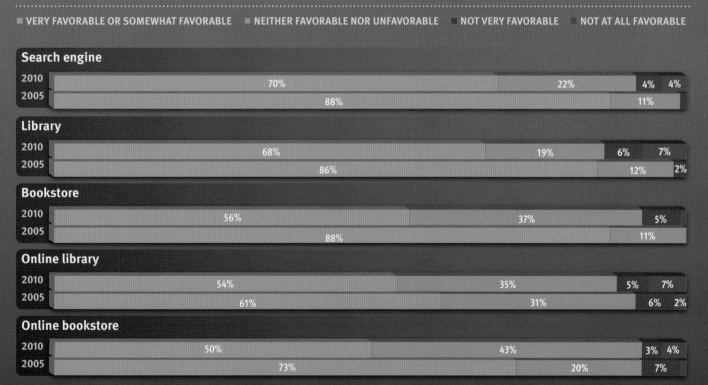

Search engine

| 2010 | 70% | 22% | 4% | 4% |
| 2005 | 88% | | 11% | |

Library

| 2010 | 68% | 19% | 6% | 7% |
| 2005 | 86% | | 12% | 2% |

Bookstore

| 2010 | 56% | 37% | 5% | |
| 2005 | 88% | | 11% | |

Online library

| 2010 | 54% | 35% | 5% | 7% |
| 2005 | 61% | 31% | 6% | 2% |

Online bookstore

| 2010 | 50% | 43% | 3% | 4% |
| 2005 | 73% | 20% | 7% | |

Profile
College Students

14% ARE ECONOMICALLY IMPACTED

68% CONSIDER THEMSELVES A READER

College students use and value libraries

Nearly three-fourths of college students have a library card. College students who have been assisted by a librarian are overwhelmingly (90%) satisfied with their experiences with librarians, and eight out of ten agree that librarians add value to their search process.

73%
HAVE A LIBRARY CARD

64%
VISIT THE PUBLIC LIBRARY ANNUALLY

71%
VISIT THE COLLEGE/UNIVERSITY LIBRARY ANNUALLY

57%
HAVE EVER USED THE LIBRARY WEB SITE

49%
ACCESS FREE INTERNET ANNUALLY AT THE LIBRARY

48%
USE A COMPUTER ANNUALLY AT THE LIBRARY

78%
BELIEVE THE LIBRARIAN ADDS VALUE TO SEARCH PROCESS

90%
ARE SATISFIED WITH OVERALL EXPERIENCE WITH LIBRARIAN

Demographics

College students made up 19% of our U.S. survey respondents. Nearly a third of them consider a public library as their primary library.

PRIMARY LIBRARY

College/university
59%

Public
31%

Community college
8%

AGE

■ 14–17 ■ 18–24 ■ 25–45 ■ 46–64

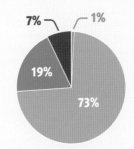

7%
1%
19%
73%

TYPE OF STUDENT

UNDERGRADUATE STUDENT 85%   GRADUATE STUDENT 15%

College Students

- Feel information from library sources is more trustworthy than search engines (43%)—more so than U.S. respondents (26%)
- Are most likely to use the library Web site (57%), and more use it weekly than in 2005 (22% up from 15%)
- Are most likely to use social networking sites (92%)
- *Begin* their online information search using search engines (83%)
- Use Wikipedia (88%)

College students are using...

99% E-MAIL

93% SEARCH ENGINES

88% WIKIPEDIA

92% SOCIAL NETWORKING SITES

81% SOCIAL MEDIA SITES

52% ASK-AN-EXPERT SITES

13% MOBILE DEVICES TO SEARCH WEB

College students advise libraries

College students want libraries to enhance their collections and to be open more hours.

29% Add or update services.

- **17%** Add/update collection
- **9%** Add/update computers
- **2%** Add programs/classes
- **1%** Make services available online

> " Improve pleasure reading collection—it is a college library that is great for research but not so well prepared for students' pleasure reading."
> **20-YEAR-OLD UNDERGRADUATE**

21% Increase customer service.

- **10%** Extend hours
- **6%** Re-examine rules
- **3%** Add staff/more knowledgeable helpful staff
- **2%** Promote the library/advertise more

> " To provide resources for people to easily access. This also includes the librarians who share their knowledge as well."
> **21-YEAR-OLD UNDERGRADUATE**

21% Improve the facility and environment.

- **10%** Renovate/expand facility
- **7%** Make finding books easier
- **4%** Study areas/meeting rooms/seating/café

> " It needs to better organize it's books and keep computers updated"
> **20-YEAR-OLD UNDERGRADUATE**

4% I'm satisfied with my library.

> " ...excellent job. "
> **20-YEAR-OLD UNDERGRADUATE**

> **More books available on a wider variety of topics."**
> 23-YEAR-OLD ECONOMICALLY IMPACTED UNDERGRADUATE

> **More computers"**
> 19-YEAR-OLD UNDERGRADUATE

> **Increase hours and days of operation"**
> 56-YEAR-OLD GRADUATE STUDENT

> **Ease up on the fees"**
> 20-YEAR-OLD UNDERGRADUATE

> **Become cooler"**
> 18-YEAR-OLD UNDERGRADUATE

> **more study rooms"**
> 23-YEAR-OLD GRADUATE STUDENT

> **it is great! "**
> 21-YEAR-OLD UNDERGRADUATE

TEENS AND YOUNG ADULTS

Teens take information habits with them as they mature

Teens continue their online information habits as they age. In 2005, teens (ages 14–17) led across all age groups in usage rates of many online resources, such as instant messaging (IM), e-journals and blogs. Teens no longer lead. That role was taken over by young adults ages 18–24—the 2005 teens. Young adults have taken their information-seeking habits with them as they aged, using these familiar tools at even greater rates.

For example, in 2005, 75% of teens and 69% of young adults used IM. Today that lead has reversed. Just 64% of teens use IM vs. 80% of young adults. Likewise, library Web site use has dropped slightly for teens from 2005 to 2010 but is up significantly, over 20%, for young adults. The same use trends hold for blogs and e-journals. Today's young adults are the heaviest users of most online resources, including search engines and e-mail. Young adults also are adopting resources that did not exist in 2005, such as social networking and Skype, at high rates.

What's next—what are teens using in 2010?

If the 2005 teens are now leading in 2010, what information resources are 2010 teens using? Social networking, mobile technologies, Wikipedia and ask-an-expert services. Teens lead all age groups in the use of ask-an-expert sites (62%) and Wikipedia (88%). They are the heaviest texters of any age group, a substitute for IM, which declined significantly from 2005.

What services are used most by young adults? The short answer is everything. Young adults showed increases in nearly all online services measured. And like teens, young adults are adopting social

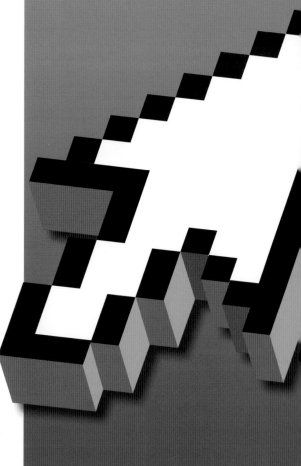

Our 2005 youth are today's young adults

Young adults' Internet behaviors show they continue to use technology they were using in their youth.

Teens
AGE 14–17

Use of electronic information sources decreases.

Young Adults
AGE 18–24

Use of electronic information sources increases.

Teens				Young Adults		
75% 2005 ▸ **64%** 2010	15% DECREASE ▼	**Instant messaging**	16% INCREASE ▲	**69%** 2005 ▸ **80%** 2010
44% 2005 ▸ **42%** 2010	5% DECREASE ▼	**Library Web site**	23% INCREASE ▲	**44%** 2005 ▸ **54%** 2010
39% 2005 ▸ **28%** 2010	28% DECREASE ▼	**Blogs**	58% INCREASE ▲	**24%** 2005 ▸ **38%** 2010
35% 2005 ▸ **20%** 2010	43% DECREASE ▼	**E-journals**	18% INCREASE ▲	**34%** 2005 ▸ **40%** 2010
18% 2005 ▸ **10%** 2010	44% DECREASE ▼	**Online databases**	17% INCREASE ▲	**24%** 2005 ▸ **28%** 2010

sites, Wikipedia and mobile Internet use. They are quickly adopting Skype, and they text though not as much as teens.

Young Americans hold library cards: 75% of teens and 68% of young adults. Two-thirds of young Americans consider themselves readers. Their top piece of advice for libraries: add or update the content.

Social

Both teens and young adults have quickly adopted social sites. Five years ago, social networking was in its infancy, and social media was just emerging. These sites are now among the most popular and frequently used online sources for teens and young adults. Three-quarters of teens (72%) and 88% of young adults use social networking sites, while 85% of teens and 88% of young adults use social media.

While e-mail remains a relevant communication tool, daily use has declined. Conversely, daily use of social networking sites increased in the last three years, as teens and young adults expanded their resources beyond e-mail and IM.

2010 results reveal new tools like Skype and Twitter as resources teens and young adults show a propensity for adopting. Skype is most popular among young adults (42%); they are twice as likely to have used Skype compared to other age groups. Twitter has been used by a quarter of those ages 14–24.

Personal phones

Cell phones have become an integral part of daily life—75% of teens ages 12–17 own a cell phone (Pew). Texting among teens has shown astonishing growth in five years. The percent who text has grown from 33% to 88% of teen cell phone users (Pew, April 2010). The amount of texting by teens (ages 13–17) is astounding—an average of 3,339 texts per month or over 100 per day (Nielsen, October 2010). Teens and young adults are also migrating Internet searching to mobile devices. Web access via mobile devices has doubled in the last five years.

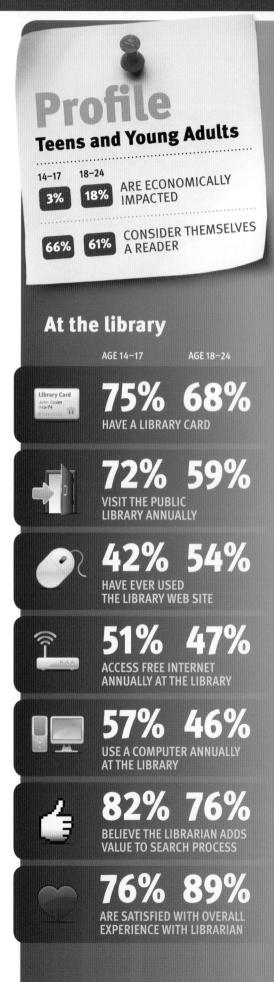

Profile

Teens and Young Adults

14–17	18–24	
3%	18%	ARE ECONOMICALLY IMPACTED
66%	61%	CONSIDER THEMSELVES A READER

At the library

AGE 14–17	AGE 18–24	
75%	68%	HAVE A LIBRARY CARD
72%	59%	VISIT THE PUBLIC LIBRARY ANNUALLY
42%	54%	HAVE EVER USED THE LIBRARY WEB SITE
51%	47%	ACCESS FREE INTERNET ANNUALLY AT THE LIBRARY
57%	46%	USE A COMPUTER ANNUALLY AT THE LIBRARY
82%	76%	BELIEVE THE LIBRARIAN ADDS VALUE TO SEARCH PROCESS
76%	89%	ARE SATISFIED WITH OVERALL EXPERIENCE WITH LIBRARIAN

Teens: 14- to 17-year-olds

- Are heaviest users of ask-an-expert sites (62%)
- Are most likely to have a library card (75%) and visit the library annually (72%)
- Are heaviest texters averaging 3,339 texts per month (Nielsen, 13–17-year-olds)

Young Adults: 18- to 24-year-olds

- Are heaviest users of the library Web site (54%)
- Report the highest growth in ask-an-expert site use (350%)
- Are most likely to use Skype (42%)

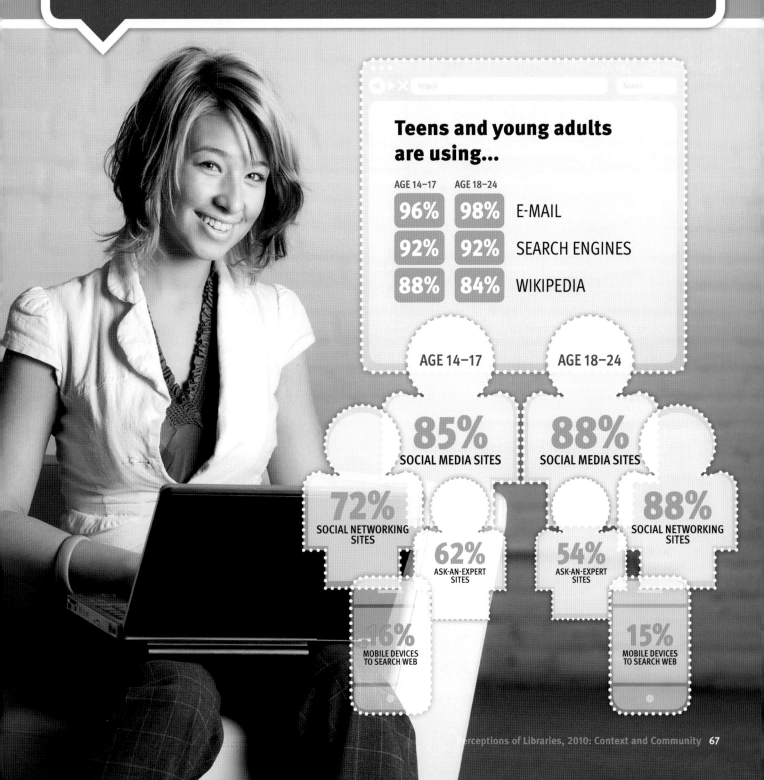

Teens and young adults are using...

AGE 14–17	AGE 18–24	
96%	98%	E-MAIL
92%	92%	SEARCH ENGINES
88%	84%	WIKIPEDIA

AGE 14–17

85%
SOCIAL MEDIA SITES

72%
SOCIAL NETWORKING SITES

62%
ASK-AN-EXPERT SITES

16%
MOBILE DEVICES TO SEARCH WEB

AGE 18–24

88%
SOCIAL MEDIA SITES

88%
SOCIAL NETWORKING SITES

54%
ASK-AN-EXPERT SITES

15%
MOBILE DEVICES TO SEARCH WEB

Teens: 14- to 17-year-olds advise libraries

Teens want libraries to update their collections.

29% Add or update services.

21% Add/update collection

5% Add/update computers

2% Make services available online

1% Add programs/classes

> " Have more computers and don't let full classes use them."
> **16-YEAR-OLD ECONOMICALLY IMPACTED**

14% Increase customer service.

7% Extend hours

3% Re-examine rules

3% Add staff/more knowledgeable helpful staff

1% Promote the library/advertise more

> " Stay open later on weekdays. It helps students out considerably."
> **16-YEAR-OLD**

11% Improve the facility and environment.

8% Renovate/expand facility

2% Make finding books easier

1% Study areas/meeting rooms/seating/café

> " Make the library a more visually appealing place."
> **16-YEAR-OLD**

6% I'm satisfied with my library.

> " It's nice."
> **16-YEAR-OLD**

> " **Get more copies of popular books.**"
> 14-YEAR-OLD ECONOMICALLY IMPACTED

> " **get more cool DVDs.**"
> 17-YEAR-OLD ECONOMICALLY IMPACTED

> " **Advertise more to the youthful generation because they are your future.**"
> 17-YEAR-OLD

> " **More teen-friendly & fun.**"
> 14-YEAR-OLD

> " **You're doing great.**"
> 17-YEAR-OLD

Young Adults: 18- to 24-year-olds advise libraries

Young adults want libraries to update their collections and their buildings.

28% **Add or update services.**

17% Add/update collection

7% Add/update computers

2% Add programs/classes

2% Make services available online

> " I would like to see them offer some interesting classes for free to the public."
> **23-YEAR-OLD**

18% **Increase customer service.**

8% Extend hours

4% Re-examine rules

3% Promote the library/advertise more

3% Add staff/more knowledgeable helpful staff

> " Do not close on holidays and early in the evening when working people are off."
> **21-YEAR-OLD ECONOMICALLY IMPACTED**

17% **Improve the facility and environment.**

10% Renovate/expand facility

4% Study areas/meeting rooms/seating/café

3% Make finding books easier

> " Some more rooms where you can talk with small groups of people."
> **18-YEAR-OLD COLLEGE UNDERGRADUATE**

6% **I'm satisfied with my library.**

> " Good Job guys."
> **23-YEAR-OLD**

> **❝ Carry more books that could benefit research.❞**
> 18-YEAR-OLD

> **❝ have more staff on hand.❞**
> 19-YEAR-OLD

> **❝ Have a pamphlet detailing how books are organized in the library.❞**
> 19-YEAR-OLD COLLEGE UNDERGRADUATE

> **❝ ...amazing work.❞**
> 21-YEAR-OLD

Generation X hardest hit by the economy

The recent recession had the greatest impact on the employment status of Generation X, Americans ages 25–45. More than a quarter (28%) experienced a negative job impact (unemployed, reemployed at a lower salary or potentially working multiple jobs to make ends meet, etc.). Generation X was also the group most likely to be laid off and still unemployed at the time of the study—with 11% unemployed.

Gen Xers have made lifestyle changes as a result of the recession. Two-thirds of them (68%) are spending less on dining out and more than half of them have reduced their spending on books, CDs and DVDs (51%) and on entertainment (60%). More than a third have had to decrease the amount they can add to their savings and retirement accounts as a result of a negative job impact. They are spending less and saving less—but they are using the library more. The top reason for their increased use of the library—to save money.

A quarter (25%) of Gen Xers—more than any other age group—have increased their use of libraries during the recession. Among those who increased their library use, borrowing books, CDs and DVDs (84%), reading magazines (35%) and attending child-related events (25%) are some activities they are doing more often.

Many Gen Xers are also using the library for the first time for technology-related needs, such as accessing free Internet (30%) and using the computer (22%). Roughly 15% of these library users are attending training or educational programs, and seeking job/ career and unemployment information for the first time due to the recession.

Generation X are most impacted by the economic downturn

28% had a negative job impact—that's 18 million Americans.

Gen Xers have increased their use of libraries during the recession more than any other age group.

Many Gen X library users are accessing free Internet (30%), using the computer (22%) and searching for job/career information (16%) at the library for the first time.

25% have increased library use

68% are spending less on dining out

51% are spending less on books, CDs, DVDs

Gen X use of online information sources soars

Generation X Americans increased their use of all online information sources from e-mail to search engines, online bookstores and library Web sites.

In 2010, Gen Xers used e-mail and search engines at rates consistent with teens and young adults. Gen Xers lagged behind the younger generations in their use of blogs and instant messaging in 2005, but their usage growth in five years now puts them ahead of teens (14–17-year-olds).

Teens and young adults were at least 50% more likely to be using social sites in 2007 compared to Gen Xers. In three years, triple-digit growth in social site use among 25–45-year-olds has narrowed that usage gap for both social networking and social media sites. Eighty percent (80%) of Americans ages 25–45 now use social networking sites—more than twice as many as in 2007 (36%), resulting in a 122% three-year growth rate and now surpassing teen use (72%).

While social media site use more than doubled from 30% to 73% in three years, Gen Xers still trail teens and young adults in their propensity to use social media sites.

Three-fourths (74%) of Generation X Americans consider themselves readers. Ninety-four percent (94%) who have been assisted by a librarian are satisfied with the support they receive from librarians. Their top piece of advice to their library: add and update the collection. Extending library hours for the convenience of working Americans also is requested.

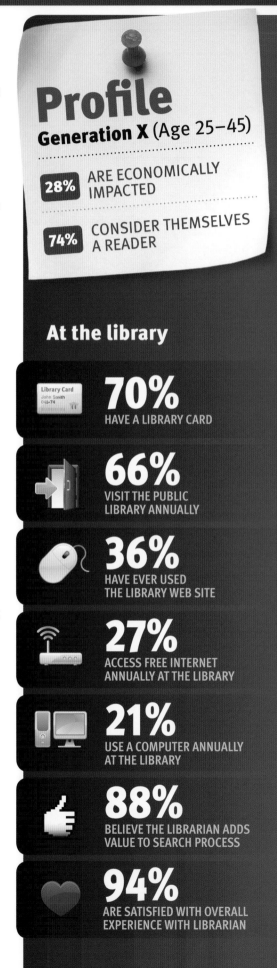

Profile
Generation X (Age 25–45)

28% ARE ECONOMICALLY IMPACTED

74% CONSIDER THEMSELVES A READER

At the library

70% HAVE A LIBRARY CARD

66% VISIT THE PUBLIC LIBRARY ANNUALLY

36% HAVE EVER USED THE LIBRARY WEB SITE

27% ACCESS FREE INTERNET ANNUALLY AT THE LIBRARY

21% USE A COMPUTER ANNUALLY AT THE LIBRARY

88% BELIEVE THE LIBRARIAN ADDS VALUE TO SEARCH PROCESS

94% ARE SATISFIED WITH OVERALL EXPERIENCE WITH LIBRARIAN

Generation X: 25- to 45-year-olds

- Are most impacted by the economy—28% have had a negative job impact
- Are most likely to have increased their library use due to the economic downturn (25%)
- Use social networking sites at rates now surpassing teens (80% vs. 72%)
- Use social networking sites at more than double the rate of three years ago (80% vs. 36%)
- Doubled their use of ask-an-expert sites in five years (39% vs. 18%)
- Are most likely to believe the librarian adds value to the search process (88%)

Generation X are using...

92% E-MAIL

93% SEARCH ENGINES

80% WIKIPEDIA

80% SOCIAL NETWORKING SITES

73% SOCIAL MEDIA SITES

39% ASK-AN-EXPERT SITES

16% MOBILE DEVICES TO SEARCH WEB

Generation X advises libraries

Gen Xers want libraries to offer more books, DVDs and other materials and to extend their hours.

23% **Add or update services.**

13% Add/update collection

6% Add/update computers

3% Add programs/classes

1% Make services available online

> " carry comic books "
> **31-YEAR-OLD**

> " More computer terminals with Internet."
> **35-YEAR-OLD ECONOMICALLY IMPACTED**

22% **Increase customer service.**

10% Extend hours

7% Re-examine rules

3% Add staff/more knowledgeable helpful staff

2% Promote the library/advertise more

> " Have extended hours at least one day per week to allow 9 to 5ers the opportunity to use the library."
> **38-YEAR-OLD**

12% **Improve the facility and environment.**

8% Renovate/expand facility

3% Make finding books easier

1% Study areas/meeting rooms/seating/café

> " Become a center for community activities."
> **45-YEAR-OLD**

> " Less Cluttered more space and light."
> **27-YEAR-OLD**

5% **I'm satisfied with my library.**

> " ...doing a great job."
> **31-YEAR-OLD**

> " Add more job skills classes."
>
> **31-YEAR-OLD COLLEGE UNDERGRADUATE**

> " The staff could be more knowledgable about the basics."
>
> **28-YEAR-OLD ECONOMICALLY IMPACTED**

> " Remodel your interior to look more modern."
>
> **24-YEAR-OLD**

> " ...it is a nice place."
>
> **45-YEAR-OLD**

BOOMERS

Closing the age divide

Five years ago, Americans ages 46–64 lagged behind younger Americans in their use of most electronic information resources. Today, Boomers' use of e-mail, search engines, blogs, instant messaging, online bookstores and online news is similar to younger information consumers. Boomers have adopted technologies at accelerating rates since 2005 and are close to eliminating the age-related digital divide.

Most Boomers now use e-mail (95%) and search engines (91%). Those using e-mail do so daily (95%) and, among search engine users, more than half search daily (57%).

Boomers report triple-digit growth of social sites

The 46–64-year-old Americans are also quickly gaining ground in the use of social sites. Half are now using social networking (52%) and social media (58%) sites, representing the age group with the highest growth in three years for social networking sites—at 247%. Behind e-mail, search engines and online news sites, social networking sites are Boomers' most frequently used online sources. Forty-three percent (43%) of Boomers who use social networking sites use them daily—two-thirds use these sites at least weekly. Social media sites gained in popularity. A third (34%) of Boomers who use social media sites use them at least monthly, while the majority use them on an "as-needed" basis (60%).

Getting answers using ask-an-expert sites increased by a triple-digit rate among American Boomers—a similar growth trend seen in all ages. Forty-two percent (42%) of Americans ages 46–64 are now using these sites—a 180% increase in usage from 15% in 2005.

> Today, Boomers' use of e-mail and search engines is similar to that of younger Americans, and Boomers are gaining ground with social networking.

Using e-mail

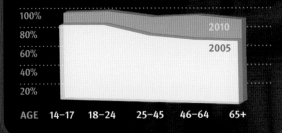

| | 2010 |
| | 2005 |

100%
80%
60%
40%
20%

AGE 14–17 18–24 25–45 46–64 65+

Using search engines

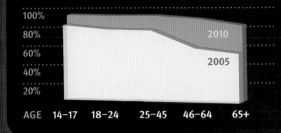

| | 2010 |
| | 2005 |

100%
80%
60%
40%
20%

AGE 14–17 18–24 25–45 46–64 65+

Using social networking sites

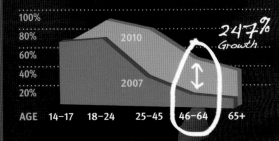

247%
Growth

100%
80%
60%
40%
20%

2010
2007

AGE 14–17 18–24 25–45 46–64 65+

Boomers report the highest growth in social networking use—**247% in three years.**

Five years later, e-mail and search engine use among Americans ages 46–64 closes the age-related digital divide.

A quarter of Boomers are impacted

Boomers were heavily affected by the recent recession. Twenty-three percent (23%) of Boomers experienced a negative change in employment status due to the economic environment. As a result, Boomers indicated significant changes in spending patterns and lifestyle choices. Boomers are the age segment reporting the largest decrease in leisure and recreational spending. Expenditures were significantly reduced on entertainment (65%) and books, CDs and DVDs (53%). They are nearly 50% more likely to have reduced spending on these leisure activities compared to younger Americans.

Like Generation X Americans, Boomers indicated double-digit increases in library use. Seventeen percent (17%) of Boomers increased their library use and the majority did so to save money by borrowing materials rather than purchasing. The vast majority of Boomers who increased their library use are borrowing books, CDs and DVDs more often (91%). Boomers have also increased their use across a broad range of library services, including using the computer (11%), accessing free Internet (21%) and Wi-Fi (11%). American Boomers are also using the library more often for job-related activities, training or educational programs, and seeking college-related information.

Boomers consider themselves to be readers (77%). They are the age group most likely to advise the library to increase customer service (33%)—in particular, to extend hours (18%).

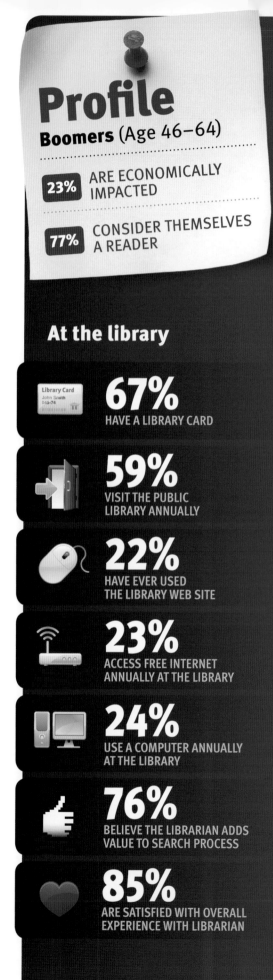

Profile
Boomers (Age 46–64)

23% ARE ECONOMICALLY IMPACTED

77% CONSIDER THEMSELVES A READER

At the library

67% HAVE A LIBRARY CARD

59% VISIT THE PUBLIC LIBRARY ANNUALLY

22% HAVE EVER USED THE LIBRARY WEB SITE

23% ACCESS FREE INTERNET ANNUALLY AT THE LIBRARY

24% USE A COMPUTER ANNUALLY AT THE LIBRARY

76% BELIEVE THE LIBRARIAN ADDS VALUE TO SEARCH PROCESS

85% ARE SATISFIED WITH OVERALL EXPERIENCE WITH LIBRARIAN

Boomers: 46- to 64-year-olds

- Reported the largest growth (247%) in social networking use in three years
- Are among the hardest hit by the economy—23% experienced a negative job impact
- Are most likely to have reduced spending on entertainment (65%) and books, CDs and DVDs (53%) due to the economic environment
- Are most likely to consider themselves a reader (77%)
- Are most likely to advise the library to extend hours (18%)

Boomers are using...

95% E-MAIL

91% SEARCH ENGINES

61% WIKIPEDIA

58%
SOCIAL MEDIA SITES

7%
MOBILE DEVICES TO SEARCH WEB

52%
SOCIAL NETWORKING SITES

42%
ASK-AN-EXPERT SITES

Boomers advise libraries

Boomers want libraries to be open more hours.

33% **Increase customer service.**

18% Extend hours

7% Re-examine rules

6% Add staff/more knowledgeable helpful staff

2% Promote the library/advertise more

> " Advertise Advertise Advertise!!!"
> **61-YEAR-OLD ECONOMICALLY IMPACTED**

17% **Add or update services.**

10% Add/update collection

4% Add/update computers

3% Make services available online

> " Secure more funding for updated books computers internet access community needs etc!"
> **46-YEAR-OLD COLLEGE UNDERGRADUATE**

11% **Improve the facility and environment.**

9% Renovate/expand facility

1% Study areas/meeting rooms/seating/café

1% Make finding books easier

> " More comfortable furniture."
> **55-YEAR-OLD ECONOMICALLY IMPACTED**

> " Remodel"
> **55-YEAR-OLD**

11% **I'm satisfied with my library.**

> " Don't change a thing!!"
> **61-YEAR-OLD**

Seniors adopt social sites

Social site use has soared among seniors. A third of American seniors (34%) now use social media sites, up from just 9% in 2007. Seniors report similar increases with social networking sites with 40% of seniors using social networking online, a 208% increase over 2007 (13%).

Getting answers using ask-an-expert sites also increased by triple-digit growth among American seniors. A third (32%) of seniors use online reference to seek assistance with their information searches, an increase of 300% from five years ago. Finding answers via ask-a-librarian question services has not taken off with seniors; use is just 3%, down slightly from 2005.

Seniors have caught up with younger Americans in their use of e-mail and search engines. Five years ago Americans ages 65+ showed substantial usage of e-mail (69%) and search engines (59%) but lagged behind younger age groups. Five years later, Americans 65+ now use e-mail (92%), search engines (86%) and other online information sources at similar or even higher rates than the younger generations.

Use of online bookstores and news sites has also increased for seniors. Today, two-thirds of seniors use online bookstores (69%) and online news sites (66%)—an increase from 41% for both sources—exceeding use among the 14–17-year-olds for online bookstores (58%) and online news sites (60%), and exceeding use among 25–64-year-olds for online news sites (64%).

Seniors' use of social sites soars

Although still behind the younger generations, seniors' use of social sites has soared in the last three years.

Social networking

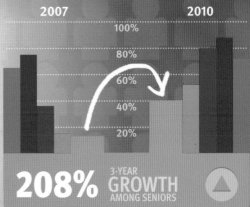

2007   2010

100%
80%
60%
40%
20%

208% 3-YEAR GROWTH AMONG SENIORS

Social media

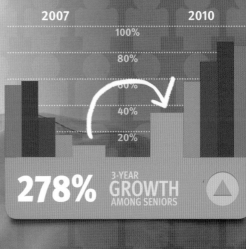

2007   2010

100%
80%
60%
40%
20%

278% 3-YEAR GROWTH AMONG SENIORS

Ask-an-expert

2005   2010

100%
80%
60%
40%
20%

300% 5-YEAR GROWTH AMONG SENIORS

- AGE 14–17
- AGE 18–24
- AGE 25–45
- AGE 46–64
- AGE 65+

Seniors have made substantial lifestyle changes

Though fewer seniors, just 7%, reported employment status impacted by the economy, they are concerned about their futures, healthcare and retirement savings and have therefore made substantial lifestyle changes due to the economy.

Most seniors are concerned about healthcare (78%), government aid (62%), finances (57%) and retirement (48%). As expected, senior Americans expressed higher levels of concern for healthcare and government aid compared to the younger generations. As a consequence, seniors have made lifestyle changes. Half of American seniors ages 65+ have reduced spending on dining out, and 40% or more of them have reduced spending on books, CDs, DVDs (40%) and entertainment (42%).

Sixteen percent (16%) of American seniors increased their library use as a result of the tough economic times. Among these library users, most (84%) are borrowing books, CDs and DVDs more often; a quarter are attending meetings/community events (26%) and reading magazines (25%); and some are attending educational training programs (18%) and accessing the Internet (16%) more often.

Seniors' top advice to libraries is to increase hours. They were the age group most likely to be satisfied with their library experience, with 14% saying no improvements to the library were needed. Senior Americans' request to libraries: "Always be there."

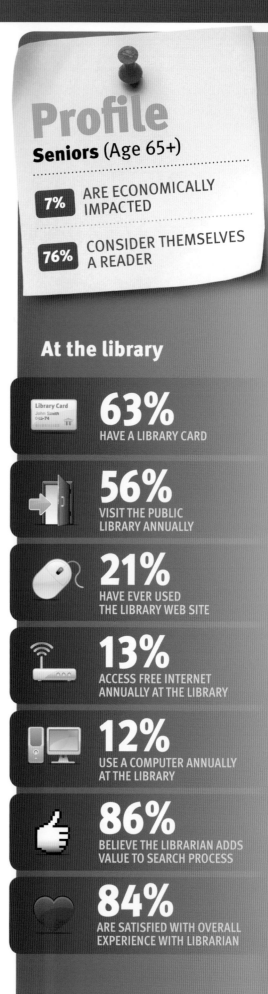

Profile

Seniors (Age 65+)

7% ARE ECONOMICALLY IMPACTED

76% CONSIDER THEMSELVES A READER

At the library

63% HAVE A LIBRARY CARD

56% VISIT THE PUBLIC LIBRARY ANNUALLY

21% HAVE EVER USED THE LIBRARY WEB SITE

13% ACCESS FREE INTERNET ANNUALLY AT THE LIBRARY

12% USE A COMPUTER ANNUALLY AT THE LIBRARY

86% BELIEVE THE LIBRARIAN ADDS VALUE TO SEARCH PROCESS

84% ARE SATISFIED WITH OVERALL EXPERIENCE WITH LIBRARIAN

Seriors: 65+-year-olds

- Had the highest growth (278%) in the use of social media sites—34% use these sites

- Are more likely to use online bookstores (69% vs. 58%) and online news sites (66% vs. 60%) compared to 14–17-year-olds

- Expressed strongest concern about healthcare (78%) and government aid (62%)

- Are most likely to say they are satisfied with the library as is when asked to provide advice to the library (14%)

Seniors are using...

92% E-MAIL

86% SEARCH ENGINES

60% WIKIPEDIA

40% SOCIAL NETWORKING SITES

34% SOCIAL MEDIA SITES

32% ASK-AN-EXPERT SITES

2% MOBILE DEVICES TO SEARCH WEB

Seniors advise libraries

Seniors are the most satisfied with the library as is, but they also want libraries to extend their hours.

23% Increase customer service.

11% Extend hours

5% Re-examine rules

4% Add staff/more knowledgeable helpful staff

3% Promote the library/advertise more

> " Better hours however with the economy I am thankful that you are there at all "
>
> **73-YEAR-OLD ECONOMICALLY IMPACTED**

15% Add or update services.

8% Add/update collection

4% Add/update computers

2% Make services available online

1% Add programs/classes

> " More large print books. "
>
> **69-YEAR-OLD**

> " Get more computers."
>
> **65-YEAR-OLD ECONOMICALLY IMPACTED**

14% I'm satisfied with my library.

> " Always be there..."
>
> **77-YEAR-OLD**

8% Improve the facility and environment.

7% Renovate/expand facility

1% Study areas/meeting rooms/seating/café

> " Our local library needs some much needed sprucing up."
>
> **71-YEAR-OLD**

> 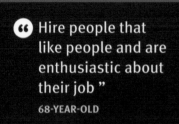 Hire people that like people and are enthusiastic about their job "
>
> 68-YEAR-OLD

> " Seek funding to ensure funding to purchase up-to-date books computers and learning materials. "
>
> 64-YEAR-OLD

> " Continue as you are."
>
> 91-YEAR-OLD

> " Put up 'street signs' for navigation"
>
> 68-YEAR-OLD

> " Nicer atmosphere."
>
> 75-YEAR-OLD ECONOMICALLY IMPACTED

GENERATIONS AT THE LIBRARY

Libraries play critical roles for Americans throughout their life stages. Whether they are checking out books, DVDs and other materials, seeking information to help revive their careers or using computer and Internet access, Americans are using libraries and find value in what libraries and librarians can do for them.

Americans who have had a negative job impact rely on the library. Eight out of ten economically impacted Americans have a library card and three-fourths of them visit the library annually. Those affected by the economy are among the most likely to see value in the library and librarians. The vast majority of economically impacted Americans believe that librarians add value to their search experience (88%) and are satisfied with their experience with librarians (92%).

Teens are among the heaviest library users. While two out of every three Americans have library cards, 75% of teens (ages 14–17) have one. The majority (62%) of Americans visit their library annually, and teens are even more likely to do so (72%). Teens are also the most likely to use the library's computer and Internet access, with more than half doing so annually.

Americans value librarians. Americans, regardless of their age, overwhelmingly believe that librarians are valuable. Across all generations and life stages, more than three-fourths of Americans who have used librarians recognize that librarians add value to their search process. And more than three-fourths of them indicate that they are satisfied with their experience with librarians. Generation X (ages 25–45) and economically impacted Americans are most likely to believe that the librarian adds value to the search process, at 88% each.

Profile

Americans at the library

20% ARE ECONOMICALLY IMPACTED

73% CONSIDER THEMSELVES A READER

HAVE A LIBRARY CARD

VISIT THE PUBLIC LIBRARY ANNUALLY

VISIT THE PUBLIC LIBRARY MONTHLY

HAVE EVER USED THE LIBRARY WEB SITE

ACCESS FREE INTERNET ANNUALLY AT THE LIBRARY

USE A COMPUTER ANNUALLY AT THE LIBRARY

BELIEVE THE LIBRARIAN ADDS VALUE TO SEARCH PROCESS

ARE SATISFIED WITH OVERALL EXPERIENCE WITH LIBRARIAN

Americans...at the library

- Two-thirds (68%) of online Americans have a library card; the majority (62%) visit the library annually
- Over 80% of Americans who use librarians believe the librarian adds value to the search process

TOTAL	ECONOMICALLY IMPACTED	COLLEGE STUDENTS	AGE 14–17	AGE 18–24	AGE 25–45	AGE 46–64	AGE 65+
68%	81%	73%	75%	68%	70%	67%	63%
62%	74%	64%	72%	59%	66%	59%	56%
28%	36%	25%	36%	23%	30%	25%	25%
33%	38%	57%	42%	54%	36%	22%	21%
28%	35%	49%	51%	47%	27%	23%	13%
27%	35%	48%	57%	46%	21%	24%	12%
83%	88%	78%	82%	76%	88%	76%	86%
87%	92%	90%	76%	89%	94%	85%	84%

■ HIGHEST PERCENTAGE FOR EACH ACTIVITY

GENERATIONS ONLINE

The majority of Americans use almost all of the online information resources examined in this study. Nearly all Americans are e-mailing and searching the Web, and many have come to rely on Wikipedia. Two-thirds of Americans use social networking and social media sites. Four out of ten Americans use ask-an-expert sites, and use of these sites has shown triple-digit growth in the last five years.

Nearly all Americans use e-mail and search engines. Nine of out ten Americans, from all age groups, use these most popular information resources. Older Americans, who in 2005 lagged behind in the use of both e-mail and search engines, now use these resources at rates similar to younger Americans.

Two-thirds of Americans use social networking sites. And college students are most likely to use them. With 92% of college students using them, social networking sites are among the most popular online resources. This finding isn't surprising considering that one of the most well-known social sites, Facebook, was open only to college students when it first launched.

Wikipedia is used by three-fourths of Americans. Although the majority of our survey respondents (51%) rate information from library sources as more trustworthy than from Wikipedia, the fact is Americans are using Wikipedia. Teens (ages 14–17) and college students are among those most likely to use Wikipedia, with 88% of both groups using it. The majority of older Americans also use Wikipedia.

Profile

Americans online

84% START THEIR INFORMATION SEARCH WITH A SEARCH ENGINE

73% USE WIKIPEDIA

USE E-MAIL

USE SEARCH ENGINES

USE WIKIPEDIA

USE ONLINE BOOKSTORES

USE SOCIAL NETWORKING SITES

USE SOCIAL MEDIA SITES

USE ASK-AN-EXPERT SITES

USE BLOGS

Americans...online

- Nearly all Americans use e-mail and search engines
- Two-thirds of Americans use social sites

TOTAL	ECONOMICALLY IMPACTED	COLLEGE STUDENTS	AGE 14–17	AGE 18–24	AGE 25–45	AGE 46–64	AGE 65+
94%	92%	99%	96%	98%	92%	95%	92%
92%	96%	93%	92%	92%	93%	91%	86%
73%	71%	88%	88%	84%	80%	61%	60%
72%	78%	78%	58%	79%	71%	75%	69%
66%	80%	92%	72%	88%	80%	52%	40%
66%	71%	81%	85%	88%	73%	58%	34%
43%	45%	52%	62%	54%	39%	42%	32%
28%	30%	38%	28%	38%	30%	27%	18%

■ HIGHEST PERCENTAGE FOR EACH ACTIVITY

A Long View— Looking Forward

Perceptions of the information consumer—2010

Economic swings do not always lead to permanent social change, but few environmental factors can create as swift a change in attitudes and practices as a severe or prolonged economic downturn. The Great Recession of the last decade has proven to be no exception. The recession had a profound impact on the actions, attitudes and values of the American information consumer, including a change in her use and perceived value of the library. Across every age group, library use increased. The perceived value of the library also increased. Library funding did not.

While the U.S. economy slowed, the pace of information technology seemed to accelerate. And with each new technology, the information consumer became more empowered. In the last five years, the Internet went from a tool for business to a social hub where we can all become friends—and share information. Social networks went from a concept to a way of life—first for the youth, now for all ages. And all the while, Google's influence grew. Most information consumers started their information searches on a search engine. In the meantime, Google scanned two trillion words, or 11% of all published books. Information consumers embraced easy-to-digest information on Wikipedia—despite the warnings of educators and librarians. Apple flourished during The Great Recession as cell phones went from being mobile phones to mobile computers. Sending over 3,000 texts a month became average for teens.

Oh, what a difference five years make. And yet, much remains the same. Libraries are even more about books. Brands are hard to change, almost impossible for a brand as strong as libraries—in an environment where saving money on books is even more valued by

2010 Hot Spots

🔥 **Libraries help users save money.** The top reason for increased library use in 2010 was to save money. Spending on books, CDs and DVDs decreased for 76% of those who experienced a negative job impact in the recession. The library filled the gap. A third of those who had a negative job impact used the library more, and 75% of them said they are now borrowing books, CDs and DVDs rather than purchasing.

🔥 **Search engines are still hot.** Information consumers continue to begin information searches on search engines. 84% of information consumers began their searches on search engines. 3% begin on Wikipedia. Not a single U.S. respondent in 2010, including college students, began an information search on a library Web site, down from 1% in 2005.

🔥 **The shine is off information resources.** Most resources, from search engines to online bookstores, are not as favorable to information consumers. Favorability ratings, while still strong, are down ten points since 2005. One exception— the favorability of library Web sites is flat.

🔥 **Search engines and libraries are trustworthy.** Search engines are used not simply because they are fast and convenient, but because they provide worthwhile, credible and free information.

Social networking is for all ages. It is no longer just a youth activity. Facebook surpassed Google as the most-visited site in March 2010. 52% of Boomers and 40% of seniors use social networking sites.

Staying connected is a priority. Information consumers will pay for access to the Internet and mobile services—they will pay to stay connected.

Information consumers are confident. They know how to find information. They will self-serve and are self-sufficient. Information consumers "just know" if information is trustworthy; they use experience and common sense as the judge. If the information found on a Web site is doubted, the information consumer will search for it on another site until satisfied.

Asking questions online grows. Use of ask-an-expert services is up 186% from 2005 (15%) to 43% in 2010. Ask-an-expert services are used by all age groups.

Ask-a-librarian services have not taken off. Five percent (5%) of information consumers used library answer services in 2005 and 7% in 2010. College student use remains low, at under 10%.

consumers. Existing brands get reinforced, not redefined, as new alternatives enter a market. Core value can be a point of strength, if recognized—and even a point of growth, if put into the new context.

Love for librarians remains. Like the library brand, it grew stronger. It seems that self-sufficient information consumers still appreciate expertise and a passion for learning—but they like it best on their time, with their tools. It's cool to ask an expert—online. It was not cool to ask a librarian for help in 1950 (Public Library Inquiry, 1950); it's still not cool.

Many more perceptions and attitudes have remained the same for the information consumer in the last five years. She still wants to self-serve and self-navigate the info sphere. She discovered the benefits of surfing the Internet by 2003 and, by 2010, was using more powerful tools. She is creating her own apps. She still knows good information when she sees it. She takes her information habits, and perceptions, with her as she ages. While she may be a bit less impressed with online information resources as they have become commonplace, nothing has yet replaced the value and speed of a search engine. And, her personal device connects her to a network where she can share the knowledge gained. She shares her info sphere with older information consumers but does not welcome information gates or gatekeepers.

Her advice for libraries: more hours, more content, more computers and of course—more books.

A Long View—into the next decade

The perceptions and beliefs of today's information consumer will shape the use, value and impact of libraries in 2011 and beyond. As libraries' budgets get tighter, expectations of the information consumer will only continue to expand. How can libraries balance the budget while balancing increased demand and new expectations? How will libraries fund the strategic investment that will be required to take the long view in difficult times? What library strategies, alternative services and advocacy activities will be required to best serve tomorrow's information consumer?

A few ideas for consideration:

Rethink online strategies—beyond the library Web site.

No information consumer started her information search on a library Web site in 2010. If the library Web site is not the first stop on the information search, but rather, one of several stops on an information consumer's search trail, or maybe not at all, what must be done to increase the touch points and invitations for the information consumer to use library resources? What has Wikipedia figured out about ease of access, language and links that library Web strategies are missing?

Sixty-eight percent (68%) of Americans have library cards. Why do only 33% of Americans use the library Web site? Rethinking online strategies with users and staff with the specific goal of serving all current cardholders could create some interesting ideas, new approaches and potential new partnerships.

The library is, in so many ways, the doorway to the communities and campuses it supports. How do the library Web site and online strategy celebrate and support community initiatives, as well as library initiatives? Do the current online strategies support the important campus and community programs as well as the libraries' offline strategies? What new online services or partnerships could better integrate online and community programs?

2010 Hot Spots

"Books" as the library brand grew even stronger. The information consumer believes that the library brand was "books" in 2005. Even more believe it is "books" in 2010. 69% said "books" was the library brand in 2005, while 75% said "books" in 2010.

The most important role the library plays is consistent for all ages except for the youngest library users. For ages 18 to 65+, the top value of the library "to me" is a place to get books, videos and music. Making information freely available is number two. For those ages 14–17, what's most important "to me" about the library is a place to read, while a place to get books, videos and music is second. College students indicate that the most important personal role for the library is also a place to get books, videos and music.

The top piece of advice for libraries in 2005 was to "add more content." The top piece of advice to libraries in 2010 is "be open." So, Americans are saying, "Please add more hours—then add more content."

Fewer seek research help. Seeking research assistance at the library fell from 39% in 2005 to 28% in 2010. Print material declined as a source for validating information: 68% in 2005 to 51% in 2010.

The online library has not become a substitute for visiting the library in person. While use of the physical library saw strong growth in 2010, the library Web site is not attracting significantly more users. Penetration is basically flat from 2005 at under 35%. The top reason for not using the library Web site remains the same as in 2005: "I didn't know it existed." The top reason given by college students: "Other sites have better information."

17% of users say that their library advertises its services.

The library's perceived value for the community increased for 31% of Americans— and even more for those who experienced a negative job impact (40%).

Librarians are valued. They're even more valued than in 2005. In 2005, 76% of information consumers who have been assisted by a librarian thought librarians add value to the search process; in 2010, this grew to 83%. The value for Americans who experienced a negative job impact was even greater—at 88%.

Embrace the brand. Extend the experience. Connect the dots.

Libraries = BOOKS. And in today's economic context, libraries also equal free books and real economic value. The number-one reason for increased library use is to save money—on books, DVDs and music.

While users increased their use of library materials, they are also discovering the many other services that libraries have to offer. These services have economic value, too. There are new opportunities to connect the dots between books and the other valuable services that the library provides that were not as readily apparent to users before the recession.

Libraries have an opportunity to create invitations to experience what comes with free book services—free job search help, free tutoring, free computer skills training, free e-books, free digital storage, etc. Existing brands get reinforced, not redefined, as new alternatives enter a market. Core value and core values are a point of strength if put into the new context of the day. Today's context is economics.

"Books" is our brand. E-books are books.

The information consumer will have every expectation that their place for books, the library, will also be their place for e-books. Existing brands get reinforced. As e-books continue to increase in use and popularity, libraries have a new opportunity to reinforce the value of the book—both the "p" and the "e" book—not either/or.

Amazon, Google and other electronic book providers will likely set the expectation for e-books—not the library. Strategies on e-book delivery and partnerships are an essential part of the long view strategy for libraries.

Not only are books being redefined, so is reading. Seventy-three percent (73%) of Americans consider themselves to be readers. It may well be the redefinition of reading, not merely the redefinition of the book, that will have the most significant impact on the role of the library. How would a new or expanded definition of the reader help inform our approach to both online and offline library services? What will summer reading programs look like in five years? What will literacy programs look like in 2015?

Advertise, please!

"The library needs to advertise its services more." This encouragement was echoed many times in the verbatim comments in the survey. Just 17% of information consumers have seen an advertisement from their library, and just 11% of college students. Those who were aware of library advertising noted that signs, flyers and promotions inside the library were the most-used methods of advertising. We know that this is not where the information consumer is looking for information.

No need to advertise books—these are well-understood—but maybe advertising is needed to promote e-books or expanded library hours.

Expand library hours online.

Use is up at the library. Use is flat on library Web site. For many libraries struggling with budget cuts, reducing physical library hours and reducing staff are difficult realities. An opportunity and a need exist to support the growing demand for library services via the online library. Our study suggests that this will not happen naturally—we have seen little movement in the last five years. This important shift will come only with more promotion and expanded access to online library services—delivered both on and off the library Web site.

While our survey found that nearly a quarter of Americans see an increased value of their library, others expressed concern that the library value had decreased for them, due to shorter hours and closed branches. Some expressed that they can no longer make the trip to a library. While the virtual library will not replace the physical services, new strategies are required to balance the budget, so we need new approaches to "library hours."

2010 Advice to Libraries

" Be more vocal to the community about what you have to offer."
24-YEAR-OLD ECONOMICALLY IMPACTED

" Better hours however with the economy I am thankful that you are there at all"
73-YEAR-OLD ECONOMICALLY IMPACTED

" advertising could be helpful people may have forgotten about the resources there"
17-YEAR-OLD

" go online and make public aware of it."
73-YEAR-OLD

" Have a better website to surf materials and either view or reserve materials online."
23-YEAR-OLD

> "We need you. Don't let them take away your funding. Fight for your existence and expansion as you are now more important than ever as a foundation for the community."
>
> 50-YEAR-OLD

> "Secure more funding for updated books computers internet access community needs etc!"
>
> 46-YEAR-OLD COLLEGE UNDERGRADUATE

> "Become a center for community activities"
>
> 45-YEAR-OLD

> "Be open more hours to serve the public"
>
> 68-YEAR-OLD ECONOMICALLY IMPACTED

> "Make it easier to get a library card."
>
> 18-YEAR-OLD

Personal information trainers

The information consumer knows good information when she sees it. She uses common sense and personal knowledge. This self-reliance to determine data quality was well established by 2005; it has been reinforced through practice.

In our 2010 survey, we asked users to share their views across a wide range of information types. Did the information consumer have a different view of information quality based on type of information? The short answer is "no." From healthcare to recreational materials, self-help, career and financial information, the information consumer had the same view—search engines are favorable compared to libraries.

If information consumers are confident about search engines, what are the best strategies to support and improve, not discourage, this self-service, self-assessment model of information literacy? A metaphor might be: how can we serve our users as personal information trainers rather than information literacy instructors? How do we help the information consumer maximize the value of search engines and other self-service models—at the point of need?

Seize the moment (to talk about future money).

As sage financial advisors will remind us, it is best to sell stock when the price (value) is high. The value of libraries is high—31% of Americans see increased value for their community, and that number is even higher (40%) for Americans who have experienced a negative job impact. Let's heed the advice and "sell" our value. A strategic priority must be to encourage our users, our students and our colleagues to tell their stories—again and again, online and in person. Let's build programs to make today's perceptions fuel tomorrow's budgets.

The third place—online.

The infosphere is social. Two-thirds of online Americans use social networking. Physical libraries are social spaces and social places. Online libraries are not. The idea of the library as the "third place" was a topic of much conversation in 2003. The idea was that Americans were looking for a place, a third place, that was not home and not work, but instead a neutral place to reflect, connect and become inspired.

What could the online "third place" look like? What services and inspiration could an online third space deliver? While many libraries now have established and modestly active Facebook and other social network programs, this must be viewed as just a first step, just one possible connection. The concept of the library as the online third place has not been "socialized" across the community. What might this mean for libraries individually? For libraries collectively? The library social network—what might be possible?

Learn from our newest library information consumers.

Twenty percent (20%) of Americans have experienced a negative job impact. A third of American families have been impacted. The survey uncovered that millions of Americans who have been impacted by the economy are using and valuing the library at an increased rate.

Twice as many Americans who have had a negative job impact are using the library daily than those who are not impacted; 50% more go weekly and 33% more go to the library monthly. While at the library, they are discovering and using many new library services for the first time. Eighty-one percent (81%) hold a library card, compared to 68% of nonimpacted Americans.

Forty percent (40%) of Americans who have been impacted by the recession see an increase in the value of the library to themselves— more than double of those not impacted. Forty percent (40%) also perceive an increased value to their community.

2010 Advice to Libraries

" Please hang in there the community needs you."
70-YEAR-OLD

" Keep helping all that come through your doors."
71-YEAR-OLD

" Keep reminding the politicians of the importance of the library to the community and the need to maintain/ increase services"
59-YEAR-OLD

" continue caring about the community's needs"
21-YEAR-OLD COLLEGE UNDERGRADUATE

" get new stuff and stay open longer"
20-YEAR-OLD ECONOMICALLY IMPACTED

> **I would provide my primary library with this one piece of advise: If they continue to serve people irregardless of their financial status they will flourish."**
>
> 18-YEAR-OLD ECONOMICALLY IMPACTED

> **get with the e-book trend"**
>
> 18-YEAR-OLD

> **Make your services more known to the community."**
>
> 24-YEAR-OLD ECONOMICALLY IMPACTED

> **Go completely digital."**
>
> 20-YEAR-OLD COLLEGE UNDERGRADUATE

> **Keep up with current technologies."**
>
> 39-YEAR-OLD ECONOMICALLY IMPACTED

For many Americans, the library experience is new or renewed. This creates a great opportunity for libraries to discover more about what is needed, what is valued and what more can be provided to a new set of users who are looking to the library as a valued community asset.

Be there.

These are indeed challenging economic times for libraries, and they are challenging economic times for library users. These times demand new experiments and new approaches as many of the traditional options are simply no longer possible—or no longer what the information consumer demands. The suggestions above are just a few of the many possible ideas that surfaced as we studied what we learned about the perceptions and habits of the 2010 information consumer. We look forward to the opportunity to explore these and many other ideas as we work together to take the long view for libraries.

The information consumer is counting on libraries to "take the long view." This was clear in the survey. The top requests for libraries in our 2010 survey: "extend hours" and "add to your collections." The challenge is to leverage the library strengths, build on the core and the brand, and to seize the moment to tell the powerful stories about the vital role of the library. As an 18-year-old information consumer told it, "[The library] is a hotspot for information and we live in an age of information so it's the place to be." Or as a 77-year old information consumer summed it up, "Always be there."

> "[The library] is a hotspot for information and we live in an age of information so it's the place to be."
>
> 18-YEAR-OLD COLLEGE UNDERGRADUATE

METHODOLOGY

OCLC commissioned Harris Interactive, Inc. to field a blind study to evaluate library resource use, perceptions and impressions of libraries, and people's preferences for using information discovery tools. We also measured the impact current economic conditions had on those preferences and perceptions. Harris drew a sample of potential respondents from the Harris Poll Online panel consisting of millions of individuals worldwide. The OCLC Market Research team analyzed and summarized survey results to produce this report.

The online survey was open to residents of Canada, the United Kingdom and the United States and was conducted in English. A total of 2,229 respondents, age 14 and older, were surveyed between January 6 and January 13, 2010.

This report summarizes findings from U.S. respondents. The collected U.S. data have an overall statistical margin of error of +/- 2.68 percent at the 95 percent confidence level for the online population in the U.S. The online population may or may not represent the general population. Based on the statistics from www.internetworldstats.com, 77% of the U.S. population have Internet access. All survey data were weighted demographically to represent the online general population for each country.

In general, question wording and issues related to conducting surveys may introduce some error or bias into opinion poll findings. A total of 100 questions were included in the survey. The survey included a series of branching questions such that a participant's response to a question could lead to a series of follow-up questions.

The survey also asked open-ended questions to ensure that respondents had the opportunity to provide input in their own words. The survey results included more than 20,000 verbatim responses, a subset of which were categorized by the OCLC Market

Total U.S. respondents

BY AGE		RESPONDENTS # OF	% OF
Age 14–17		234	18%
Age 18–24		353	26%
Age 25–45		176	13%
Age 46–64		196	15%
Age 65+		375	28%

Percentage of U.S. population with Internet access

310,232,863
POPULATION (2010 EST.)

239,232,863
INTERNET USERS

12%
USER GROWTH (2005–2010)

Source: www.internetworldstats.com

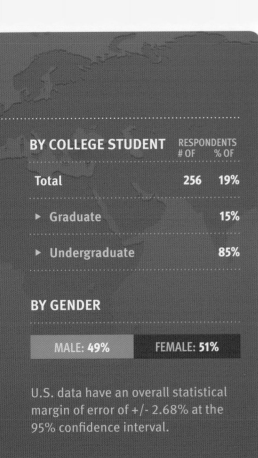

BY COLLEGE STUDENT

	RESPONDENTS # OF	% OF
Total	256	19%
▶ Graduate		15%
▶ Undergraduate		85%

BY GENDER

MALE: 49%	FEMALE: 51%

U.S. data have an overall statistical margin of error of +/- 2.68% at the 95% confidence interval.

Population with Internet access in 2010
(% of population)

77.3%

Research team and presented in this report. Verbatim responses from questions are also presented throughout the report. All verbatim comments are presented as entered by survey respondents, including spelling, grammatical and punctuation errors.

Respondents were asked to identify the library that they use primarily (e.g., public, college/university, community college, school, corporate, other) and were asked to answer all library-related question with that library in mind.

"College students" is used in the report to refer to postsecondary students, both graduate and undergraduate, responding to the survey.

The survey results are also reported by employment status in some instances, comparing those who have had a negative impact in their employment status during the recession to those who reported no changes. "Economically Impacted" is defined as those who reported a negative impact in their employment status, based on a roll-up of respondents who answered the question, "What changes have occurred in your employment status due to the current economic environment?" with any of the following responses:

- Laid off from job and still unemployed
- Laid off from job and took another job with lower pay
- Laid off from job and took another job with similar or higher pay
- Received a reduction in pay at current employer
- Have had to work more than one job to make ends meet
- Have had to increase hours of work to make ends meet
- Reentered the work force (e.g., retired, stay-at-home parent, student, etc.) to make ends meet.

"Not Impacted" is defined as those respondents who responded "No changes."

OCLC RESEARCH AND REPORTS

Read more in-depth studies and topical surveys that help you understand issues and trends that affect librarianship as you plan for the future.

Geek the Library, a community awareness campaign, is aimed at educating the community about the value of public libraries and to start funding conversations. The *Geek the Library: A Community Awareness Campaign* report (2011) documents the results of the Geek the Library pilot campaign conducted in partnership with nearly 100 public libraries in Georgia, Illinois, Indiana, Iowa and Wisconsin. The findings suggests that Geek the Library can change perceptions about libraries, librarians and public library funding, and that implementation of the campaign can positively impact public library funding trends.

TO ACCESS THE REPORT, VISIT THE OCLC WEB SITE AT:
www.oclc.org/reports/geekthelibrary.htm

How Libraries Stack Up: 2010 examines the economic, social and cultural impact of libraries in the United States. As the current economic environment is impacting library budgets and library usage is increasing, particular attention is paid to the role that libraries play in providing assistance to job-seekers and support for small businesses. Information includes statistics on libraries as providers of: job-seeking and career help; assistance to small businesses; and free community services such as Wi-Fi access, technology training and meeting rooms.

TO ACCESS THE REPORT, VISIT THE OCLC WEB SITE AT:
www.oclc.org/report/stackup

The *From Awareness to Funding: A study of library support in America* (2008) report summarizes findings from research to explore attitudes and perceptions about library funding and to evaluate the potential of a marketing campaign to increase public library funding. This report provides valuable insights into the connection between public perceptions and library support. The OCLC Geek the Library public awareness campaign grew out of this same research.

TO ACCESS THE REPORT, VISIT THE OCLC WEB SITE AT:
www.oclc.org/reports/funding

OCLC is a nonprofit membership organization that promotes cooperation among libraries worldwide. Working together, OCLC and its member libraries produce and maintain WorldCat, which now contains over 200 million bibliographic records and more than 1.6 billion library holdings. In addition to the many services offered, OCLC funds library advocacy programs that are part of a long-term initiative to champion libraries to increase their visibility and viability within their communities. Programs include market research reports that identify and communicate trends of importance to the library profession. OCLC is headquartered in Dublin, Ohio, U.S., and has offices throughout the world.

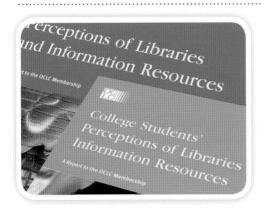

Sharing, Privacy and Trust in Our Networked World (2007) is based on a survey (by Harris Interactive on behalf of OCLC) of the general public from six countries—Canada, France, Germany, Japan, the U.K. and the U.S.— and of library directors from the U.S. The research provides insights into the values and social networking habits of library users and explores the web of social participation and cooperation on the Internet and how it may impact the library's role.

TO ACCESS THE REPORT, VISIT THE OCLC WEB SITE AT:
www.oclc.org/reports/sharing/

The ***Perceptions of Libraries and Information Resources*** (2005) and ***College Students' Perceptions of Libraries and Information Resources*** (2006) reports summarize findings of an international study on information-seeking habits and preferences. The study was conducted to learn more about: library use; awareness and use of library electronic resources and Internet search engines; use of free vs. for fee information; and the 'Library' brand.

TO ACCESS THE REPORT, VISIT THE OCLC WEB SITE AT:
www.oclc.org/reports/2005perceptions.htm
www.oclc.org/reports/perceptionscollege.htm

The 2003 OCLC Environmental Scan: Pattern Recognition was published in January 2004 for OCLC's worldwide membership to examine the significant issues and trends impacting OCLC, libraries, museums, archives and other allied organizations, both now and in the future. The Scan provides a high-level view of the information landscape, intended both to inform and stimulate discussion about future strategic directions.

TO ACCESS THE REPORT, VISIT THE OCLC WEB SITE AT:
www.oclc.org/reports/2003escan.htm

Amazon. July 19, 2010. "Kindle Device Unit Sales Accelerate Each Month in Second Quarter; New $189 Price Results in Tipping Point for Growth." [Press release] http://phx.corporate-ir.net/phoenix.zhtml?c=176060&p=irol-newsArticle&ID=1449176&highlight=

Amazon. October 25, 2010. "New Generation Kindle Device Sales Already Surpass Fourth Quarter 2009—The Peak Holiday Shopping Season and Busiest Time of Year on Amazon." [Press release] http://phx.corporate-ir.net/phoenix.zhtml?c=176060&p=irol-newsArticle&ID=1486648&highlight=

American Library Association (ALA). 2006. *Libraries Connect Communities: Public Library Funding & Technology Access Study* 2006–2007. http://www.ala.org/ala/research/initiatives/plftas/previousstudies/0607/index.cfm.

American Library Association (ALA). April 2010. *The State of America's Libraries*. http://www.ala.org/ala/newspresscenter/mediapresscenter/americaslibraries/ALA_Report_2010-ATI001-NEW1.pdf.

American Library Association (ALA). June 2010. *Libraries Connect Communities 3: Public Library Funding & Technology Access Study* 2009–2010. http://www.ala.org/ala/research/initiatives/plftas/index.cfm.

Association of American Publishers. December 2010. "AAP Reports October Book Sales." [Press release] Association of American Publishers, December 8, 2010. http://publishers.org/main/PressCenter/Archicves/2010_Dec/AAPReportsOctoberBookSales.htm.

Bernstein Research. October 2010. "iPad Adoption Rate Fastest Ever, Passing DVD Player." By John Melloy. *CNBC News*. http://www.cnbc.com/id/39501308/iPad_Adoption_Rate_Fastest_Ever_Passing_DVD_Player.

Broadcast Music Inc. (BMI). March 2008. "Ringback Tones Lead Mobile Music Market Growth in '08." http://www.bmi.com/news/entry/536285.

Burson-Marsteller Blog. September 2010. "The State of Mobile Communication." By Ashley Welde. http://www.burson-marsteller.com/Innovation_and_insights/blogs_and_podcasts/BM_Blog/Lists/Posts/Post.aspx?ID=208.

Business Wire, December, 2010. "Moosylvania Study Reveals the Top 10 Mobile Apps in the U.S. and What to Know Before You Create One." http://www.businesswire.com/news/home/20101201005326/en/Moosylvania-Study-Reveals-Top-10-Mobile-Apps.

CNET News, October 25, 2010. "Android Market Tops 100,000 Applications." By Tom Krazit. http://news.cnet.com/8301-30684_3-20020616-265.html.

comScore. August 2006. "comScore Media Metrix Search Engine Ratings." http://searchenginewatch.com/2156431.

comScore. March 2008. "Happy Anniversary, M:Metrics!" [Press release] http://comscore.com/Press_Events/Press_Releases/2008/03/M_Metrics_Anniversary/%28language%29/eng-US.

comScore. September 2010. "U.S. Smartphone Penetration by Age." http://www.comscoredatamine.com/2010/09/u-s-smartphone-users-by-age/.

comScore. December 21, 2010. "comScore Media Metrix Ranks Top 50 U.S. Web Properties for November 2010." [Press release] http://www.comscore.com/Press_Events/Press_Releases/2010/12/comScore_Media_Metrix_Ranks_Top_50_U.S._Web_Properties_for_November_2010.

Unless otherwise noted, the data points presented in this report result from the OCLC
Market Research team's analysis of the OCLC-commissioned survey results.

Other sources were also consulted throughout our research efforts as noted throughout
the report; those sources are cited here.

comScore. December 15, 2010. "comScore Releases November 2010 U.S. Search Engine Rankings." [Press release]
http://www.comscore.com/Press_Events/Press_Releases/2010/12/comScore_Releases_November_2010_U.S._Search_
Engine_Rankings.

CTIA. June 2010. "U.S. Wireless Quick Facts." http://www.ctia.org/media/industry_info/index.cfm/AID/10323.

Gerzema, John and Michael D'Antonio. 2010. *Spend Shift: How the Post-Crisis Values Revolution is Changing the Way We Buy, Sell, and Live*. San Francisco: Jossey-Bass, 2010.

Global Entrepreneurship Monitor. 2010. *Global Entrepreneurship Monitor, 2009 Global Report*. By Niels Bosma and Jonathan Levie.
http://www.gemconsortium.org/.

Hitwise Intelligence, March 2010. "Facebook Reaches Top Ranking in US." By Heather Dougherty.
http://weblogs.hitwise.com/heather-dougherty/2010/03/facebook_reaches_top_ranking_i.html.

Institute of Museum and Library Services (IMLS). 2003–2008. Library Statistics Program. http://harvester.census.gov/imls/index.asp.

Internet World Stats. September 2010. "Internet Usage Statistics for the Americas." http://www.internetworldstats.com/stats2.htm.

Library Journal. October 2010. "Gone Mobile? (Mobile Libraries Survey 2010)." By Lisa Carlucci Thomas.
http://www.libraryjournal.com/lj/communityacademiclibraries/886987-265/gone_mobile_mobile_libraries_survey.html.csp.

Morgan Stanley Research. June 2010. "Internet Trends 2010." http://www.slideshare.net/CMSummit/ms-internet-trends060710final.

Mortgage Bankers Association, 2009. *National Delinquency Survey, Fourth Quarter 2009*.

National Bureau of Economic Research. September 2010. Announcement of June 2009 business cycle trough/end of last recession.
http://www.nber.org/cycles/sept2010.html.

National Center for Education Statistics (NCES). 2003–2008. Library Statistics Program. http://nces.ed.gov/surveys/libraries/.

The New York Times. March 11, 2009. "'Great Recession': A Brief Etymology." By Catherine Rampell.
http://economix.blogs.nytimes.com/2009/03/11/great-recession-a-brief-etymology/?pagemode=print.

The New York Times. December 16, 2010. "In 500 Billion Words, New Window on Culture." By Patrica Cohen.
http://www.nytimes.com/2010/12/17/books/17words.html.

Nielsen. October 2010. "U.S. Teen Mobile Report: Calling Yesterday, Texting Today, Using Apps Tomorrow."
http://blog.nielsen.com/nielsenwire/online_mobile/u-s-teen-mobile-report-calling-yesterday-texting-today-using-apps-tomorrow/.

OCLC. 2003. *Environmental Scan: Pattern Recognition*. By Cathy De Rosa et al.

OCLC. 2005. *Perceptions of Libraries and Information Resources: A Report to the OCLC Membership*. By Cathy De Rosa et al.

OCLC. 2007. *Sharing, Privacy and Trust in Our Networked World: A Report to the OCLC Membership*. By Cathy De Rosa et al.

OCLC. 2010. *How Libraries Stack Up, 2010: A Report to the OCLC Membership*.

Pew Research Center. October 2009. "College Enrollment Hits All-Time High, Fueled by Community College Surge." By Richard Fry. http://pewresearch.org/pubs/1391/college-enrollment-all-time-high-community-college-surge.

Pew Research Center. April 2010. "Teens and Mobile Phones." By Amanda Lenhart, Rich Ling, Scott Campbell, and Kristen Purcell. http://www.pewinternet.org/Reports/2010/Teens-and-Mobile-Phones.aspx?r=1.

Public Library Inquiry. 1950. *The Public Library in the United States.* By Robert D. Leigh.

United States Courts. August 17, 2010. "Bankruptcy Filings Up 20 Percent in June." http://www.uscourts.gov/News/NewsView/10-08-17/Bankruptcy_Filings_Up_20_Percent_in_June.aspx.

U.S. Bureau of Labor Statistics. April 2010. "College Enrollment Up Among 2009 High School Grads." *TED: The Editor's Desk.* http://data.bls.gov/cgi-bin/print.pl/opub/ted/2010/ted_20100428.htm.

U.S. Bureau of Labor Statistics. October 2010. "Consumer Expenditures – 2009." http://www.bls.gov/news.release/cesan.nr0.htm.

U.S. Bureau of Labor Statistics. January 2011. "Employment, Hours and Earnings from the Current Employment Statistics Survey." http://data.bls.gov:8080/PDQ/outside.jsp?survey=ce.

U.S. Census Bureau. June 2010. "Annual 2009 Characteristics of New Housing." http://www.census.gov/const/www/charindex.html#singlecomplete.

USA Today. January 2011. "Week after holidays, e-book sales outdo print." http://www.usatoday.com/life/books/news/2011-01-05-1Aebooksales05_ST_N.htm.

Wall Street Journal. September 9, 2010. "Google's New Features Designed to Speed Web Searches." By Amir Efrati. http://online.wsj.com/article/SB10001424052748703453804575479821579919484.html.

Wells Fargo/Gallup Small Business Index. August 2010. "Wells Fargo/Gallup Small Business Index Hits New Low in July." By Dennis Jacobe. http://www.gallup.com/poll/141692/Wells-Fargo-Gallup-Small-Business-Index-Hits-New-Low-July.aspx.

Wireless and Mobile News. October 2010. "Facebook Top Social Media in World & U.S., Says comScore." http://www.wirelessandmobilenews.com/2010/10/facebook-top-social-media-in-world-us-says-comscore.html.